BURIED ALIVE

A Miracle Journey Of Healing
From Borderline Personality Disorder

JODIE SMITH

Buried Alive
A Miracle Journey of Healing

By: Jodie Smith

ISBN-13: 978-1984390332
ISBN-10: 1984390333

All scripture quotations in this book are from the New King James Version of the Bible unless otherwise noted.

Edited by Patricia Bollmann
For information, to schedule speaking events, or to order books by Jodie Smith, please communicate by email to
Jsmithstilllaughing@yahoo.com.

Dedication

I lovingly dedicate this book to my faithful, consistent, and loving husband, Scott. This book would never have been written without your gentle encouragement and the confidence you showed in me.

Contents

Foreword

My wife and I have been privileged to know Jodie Smith for thirty years. I will never forget the first time we saw her at our new church where we had just been elected as pastor. It was Sunday morning before church time, but there she was along with her four stair-step sons, ages ten on down to four, all sitting like ducks in a row on the front pew. The boys' hair was combed, they were wearing neckties and white shirts, and they listened and watched intently as their mom went over a special song with someone in preparation for the church service.

It wasn't long until Jodie fell in love with our youth pastor, Scott Smith. They were soon married and then, after a few years, they became pastor of the church in Blue Springs. God then blessed them with two children of their own. We have remained close friends throughout the years and have celebrated God's blessings in each of our ministries.

One of the most difficult situations I have ever been in was the day Jodie came to my office with one of her sons to tell me her marriage was in trouble and that her husband had resigned from being pastor. The very next day her husband came to my office overwhelmed with grief and pain.

After praying and crying with both of them, and after hearing both sides of the story, I was doubtful the marriage would ever survive. I'm so thrilled to be able to say that I have personally witnessed one of the greatest miracles I have ever seen in the full restoration of their marriage and ministry.

That's the good news. The bad news is that we did not know at the time we were dealing with Borderline Personality Disorder. However, after official diagnosis, countless hours of counseling, prayer, honesty, and willingness to do the heavy lifting, Jodie has taken charge of her life, and their marriage is stronger than ever.

This story is true but painful. Satan knows that if he can offend children, they will struggle their entire lives unless they receive the healing and transforming power of Jesus Christ. It is only by the grace of God, the expert care of Spirit-filled professionals, and the patience and understanding of her husband that Jodie is alive and able to tell her story.

Chances are you know someone who may have suffered innocently at the hands of the guilty, causing pain and unexplainable disruption to their life and relationships. Perhaps Jodie's story is your story. May you find solace and hope as you read the pages of this compelling story, knowing that what God has done for her, He can and will do for others.

–Stan Gleason, UPCI Assistant General Superintendent

Introduction

My heart's desire in writing this book is to help someone who has lost their way in life, whether it's a person with Borderline Personality Disorder or a caregiver. By "lost," I mean you are doing everything you know to do, but something is still wrong and you don't know how to fix it.

I don't want anyone else to go another day without a shred of hope. I know what it's like to be buried alive in a grave of hopelessness. I have endured many hours of mental torment, not knowing which way to turn. I pray that as you read this book, if you see yourself, please don't deny it. Acknowledging it is the first step toward freedom. I'm writing because I want you to find that freedom. I want you to know there is hope; there is healing; there is a bright future waiting for you. God is a God of miracles. And if He could heal someone like me, He can heal you too.

If you are the caregiver of a Borderline and living a nightmare every day not knowing what to do or how to control the emotions this person pulls from deep within your spirit, I want to bring hope to you as well. Understanding what you're dealing with is the first step toward a new future for both of you.

To God be all glory and honor.

Chapter 1

I'm Done, and It's Over!

Journal: *I'm so panic stricken I want to run away and isolate myself. I've got to protect myself.*

I pushed through the front door of our house, slamming it behind me. It was a cold, unforgiving day, and I needed to get away. Life couldn't go on like this. I was done. It was over. I had to get out of this maze and find some peace of mind.

Where am I going? What am I doing? What am I thinking? Oh God, I can't even think!

I jumped in the car and started driving. Where was I going? Everywhere. Anywhere. I didn't know. I couldn't seem to put two sentences together, enough to get across to anyone what I was thinking.

My cell phone started to ring. I pulled into a store parking lot and stared down at the screen. The phone rang and rang and finally stopped. Why wouldn't they just leave me alone? I knew this person loved and cherished me, but all I wanted was quiet and peace of mind. Was that too much to ask? When I was like this, I couldn't even think, much less process what someone else was trying to tell me.

In the momentary quiet, the phone started ringing again, and this time I answered between sobs, sighs, and groans that issued from deep within.

As countless times in the past, nothing came out of this conversation. There was no communication. I wasn't making any sense. I prayed, *Oh, God, help me!* No one but God could help me when I was like this. The feeling was just as terrifying as going over Niagara Falls. *Please help me, someone—anyone!* I was tumbling over and over, my head hitting every jagged rock. Was I bleeding? Was that blood running down the side of my face? When would I hit bottom? *Oh, God, help me!*

In the midst of this turmoil I suddenly remembered it was Wednesday night—church night. I had to pick up the kids on my church bus route, kids that I loved so dearly. I had been driving the bus for several years now. The kids were my heartbeat. After negotiating the bus route, I somehow had to teach the junior high class. My mind was a blank. How was I ever going to manage? I couldn't even seem to get myself started, much less manage a roomful of young teenagers. I made a snap decision to run by Hobby Lobby and try to find something that would spark an idea of what to teach. I paced up and down the aisles, tears still streaming down my face, trying to gather the thoughts racing through my head so I could come up with some kind of lesson.

As I finally reached my house and slowly pulled into the driveway, I was clearly a basket case. I managed to get into the house and climb the stairs, still unable to think straight. I reached my room and looked into the mirror. The woman I saw staring back at me was a total wreck. What did other people think about me? All of this had to be a sick joke. I knew there was no way I was ever going to make it through this life. *God, please help me to think of something positive.* Was there any hope that He would answer? That He would send help?

I didn't know how I was ever going to pull this off. How could I possibly walk through those church doors and look and act as if nothing was wrong? When I arrived at church, my swollen, tear-stained face would tell it all. None of this was believable to me, so how could I expect anyone else to believe it? I mean, really; did I look as if I felt well? No. I hardly ever felt well, and I sensed my problems issued from the depths of something sick, something almost sinister, inside me.

What is Borderline Personality Disorder (BPD)? In the simplest of terms, this disorder pushes a person to the edge or border of something. However, BPD does not progress to schizophrenia. It is an independent disorder with its own symptoms and prognosis. The official diagnostic criteria of the *American Psychiatric Association Manual* require a person to have five or more of the following symptoms before a diagnosis of BPD can be made.

1. Frantic efforts to avoid real or imagined abandonment
2. A pattern of unstable and intense interpersonal relationships
3. An unstable sense of self and identity

10

4. Impulsive actions that are ultimately self-damaging such as drug abuse, excessive spending, reckless driving, or unsafe sex
5. Recurrent suicidal actions, threats, thoughts, or self-injury behaviors (such as cutting)
6. Unstable, intense moods or emotions that can be triggered by events and may last hours or days
7. Chronic feelings of emptiness, boredom, or loneliness
8. Inappropriate or intense anger that is difficult to control
9. Temporary, stress-triggered, paranoid ideas ("I feel threatened by others") or severe dissociative symptoms ("I don't feel real")

BPD manifests in diverse ways according to each individual who suffers from it, because everyone has had different experiences that can trigger it. It depends largely on the type of trauma and surroundings in which they grew up.

I walked into my classroom that night feeling as if I were clinging to the edge of a cliff. Although I didn't know it, this was the last time I would ever walk through the front doors of the Lakeview church as "the pastor's wife."

I feared the kids would take one look and see right through me. Would they see I was distraught and my heart in pure agony? Around thirty-five kids came to class that night. I greeted each of them as they entered the classroom, trying to hide the feeling that I couldn't function or even think. After some small talk I headed for the light switch; I craved the dark. Number one, I knew I was falling apart. Maybe my mind was going, and I didn't want the kids to sense it. Number two, the dark would keep them quiet and they would be easier to handle. I just needed somehow to get through this lesson and then take my bus kids home. I would then try to make some sense out of this horrendous, unforgettable night. If only I could go home and fall asleep, and

> I was falling apart. Maybe my mind was going, and I didn't want the kids to sense it. I just needed somehow to get through this lesson.

never have to think about this agonizing night again. *God, I just need some peace and comfort for my weary mind.*

It was the last lesson I would ever teach to my kids. Some say you can turn any bad life experiences (divorce, abuse, molestation, jail time, etc.) into a golden nugget. But where was my golden nugget? Where had I gone wrong? I didn't understand any of it. All I knew was that if I could get through this lesson, God would somehow anoint His Word. *God, can You use someone as bad off as me to reach these desperate kids?*

As I taught, warm tears streamed down my face and dripped off my chin. What was that noise? Oh, yes! It was the quiet sobs coming from some of my students as they felt the power of God. At least I hoped that was what they were feeling. I myself couldn't think or make sense of my life—or anything else for that matter.

As I taught, I moved around the room, touching a shoulder, wiping a tear off a cheek, tucking a girl's hair behind her ears as she cried, all the while assuring them they could climb any mountain, swim any ocean, make it through any abuse that had been dealt to them in life—but only through the help of our God. Who was I to tell them they could do all these things when I didn't think I would make it through the night?

I believed what I was saying; I'd heard it taught all my life and had seen it help other people, but as for me, when would my ship come in and carry me away to safety and the peace I so desperately craved?

As I walked through the room, I placed a golden nugget on each student's lap, praying, "God, please help them to find their golden nugget. Help them to open their hearts to You, because You, God, are all most of these kids will ever have. My God, please help my kids!"

The classroom was full of kids who had no hope outside of God. I had picked up many of them while their parents were being busted for drugs. They would get in the van with tears in their eyes, telling me, "They're taking my daddy [and/or] mommy to jail." Many of them would come out half dressed, while Mommy and Daddy lay on the couch in a drunken stupor. Many of them smelled as if they hadn't bathed in weeks. Oh, how my heart ached for these children I had mentored. Many of them thought of me as a surrogate mother.

None of my kids must know their teacher felt as hopeless as they did. They thought I had everything together and owned everything I needed. Yes, I really did have everything I needed, but I hadn't learned the proper way to use it. Even as a child I had been unable to process experiences, and I still couldn't process properly. I was truly stuck in a maze and couldn't find any way out. The kids thought I had all the answers to life. If only I did . . . then maybe I could figure out mine.

I didn't know I was facing several intense, grueling years of my life, during which I would finally identify the culprit, the source of my unhealthy, mixed-up thinking process. Only then could I see the horrifying decisions I had made during those awful months. I knew I would have to relearn life all over again.

> I didn't know I was facing several intense, grueling years of my life.

At the time, though, all I knew was that I really needed God to fix my mixed-up thinking. He alone knew about my problem; nobody else had a clue. Sometimes I thought I was right and everyone else was wrong. It wasn't until much later I found out how wrong I was! Would God be able to turn my problems into a golden nugget, as I had taught my students? But somehow I knew it wouldn't be easy or pleasant. It takes a hot fire to refine gold; it takes dying as we have never died before.

After dropping off my last bus kid, I slowly made my way back to the church parking lot and parked the church van, unaware that it was the last time I would ever follow that bus route. Getting into my car, my mind was so confused that I felt disconnected from life itself. It felt almost as if I was being sifted like flour.

What was life anyway? I felt totally worthless and longed to be free of the pain and torment in my mind. But where does one go to get that freedom? And how does one accomplish it? For me, it would be easier to fall into a deep sleep and never wake up.

With a tear-stained face I at last crawled under the covers, keeping all of the turmoil to myself, locked up in my own lonely world. When would it ever end? When would I find the inner peace and joy I was supposed to have as a child of God? I had heard it preached all my life, but somehow I had missed out. *Come back here, please*, I pleaded silently. But who would hear my plea?

13

It was a long night without much sleep. I couldn't stop the thoughts that raced through my mind. Finally the timid rays of morning peered through the window, and my spirit made a feeble attempt to rise as well . . . maybe this new day would bring hope and warmth to my soul.

God, You've got to help me! I don't know how to help myself. I can't see my way out of this maze. No matter which way I turn, I run into a barrier, and there are no doors. Where are the doors, God? Or even a window? If I could find a window, I could climb out or at least lean on the ledge to get some brief moments of fresh air and peace.

Fearful of the dark, I got up and crept down the shadowy hallway. I sensed something lurking in the darkness, ready to jump out and scare me. The devil loves darkness; it's his favorite time to overload a person's mind with horrible doubts and fears. Sometimes the fear would shake every fiber in my body. As I walked down the hallway, I could almost feel him breathing down my neck, saying, "There's no hope for you, Jodie!" Exhausted, I turned, hurried back down the hallway, crawled into bed, and curled up like a baby.

> God, You've got to help me! I don't know how to help myself. No matter which way I turn, I run into a barrier.

During times of stress, some people with BPD will lean toward self-centeredness and become manipulative. Others will experience intense anger, depression, and suicidal thoughts. At times this was a description of me. After experiencing stress, I would lie for hours and sometimes days, not wanting to go on living. I would get stuck in an awful box of anger and be unable to scrabble up and out. I didn't want to be like this. I even questioned why I had been born. Some nights I would take a double or triple dose of Benadryl, thinking it would make me feel better. It would, at the very least, give me a long, much-needed sleep; maybe I would never have to wake up . . .

Opening my eyes to face another day, I usually felt like I had gone through a spin cycle—totally wrung out. What was I going to do and where was I going to go? I had no purpose that day except to breathe and merely exist. There wasn't much sense to be made out of anything. All I wanted was to fall back to sleep.

Everything after lunch was a downward spiral in a well so deep it seemed to have no bottom. Once I jumped in, there was no going back. It was the first of many bad decisions I would make in the next several months. It was as though I had fallen down a hole into another world, never to find my way back.

My mind spun out of control on fast forward . . .

One major symptom of BPD is racing thoughts, a condition that is almost indescribable. Thoughts whiz around in your mind twenty-four seven, and, unfortunately, all of them are negative. The worst thing about this is that the Borderline believes them. They are trapped in their faulty thinking and there's no way to get loose.

Another cruel, unhealthy symptom of BPD is a term called "splitting." An example of this would be, "So-and-so is either ALL good or ALL bad." One day you might think highly of your loved one or friend; all you can see is good. Then the very next day when they disappoint you, as we all do sometimes, you immediately relegate them to the all-bad side. You despise them and can't find anything good about them. It's a matter of being unable to look at the whole person with some great qualities but also some faults and weaknesses.

You can see how difficult communication would be for people with BPD. A good, honest discussion is impossible. They see themselves as either all good or all bad depending on their emotions at the time. Sometimes they really hate themselves. They feel alone and bereft of even a smidgeon of self-confidence. There's no hope.

Additionally, it's very hard for someone with BPD to accept criticism. They will react angrily and feel compelled to tell you how good they really are. It's your fault if you don't see it.

Another BPD symptom is "Everyone is against me!" They are looking through a lens riddled with ugly spots, chips, and smudges. This attitude certainly caused many misunderstandings throughout my life. I believed with all my heart, soul, and mind that *I was a victim*.

That cold, winter day I walked out of the front door of my house, not realizing I would never return to permanently live there. I walked away from everything I knew, everything I was a part of. I didn't realize I was making a decision that would affect everything connected to me. It altered my whole world, including my family: my sweet husband, Scott (pastor of Lakeview Church, presbyter, and director of men's ministry), plus my six children and six grandchildren, my parents, in-laws, and siblings. My world was forever changed. Nothing would ever be the same again.

> That cold, winter day I walked away from everything I knew, everything I was a part of. I didn't realize that I was making a decision that would affect everything connected with me.

A Borderline has grown up with so much pain and instability, the only way they know how to deal with it is to block it out. This is why they pick fights with the people closest to them and disrupt any positive or good time they may have had. As Joseph Santoro notes in his book *The Angry Heart*, life for the Borderline child is never safe or stable for very long. As soon as it seems safe, the rug is pulled out from under them. So to protect themselves they develop an "adaptive reflex" in which they learn to anticipate disaster. Oddly, this reflex becomes the only thing that eases the horrible anxiety of impending disappointment or trauma that surely awaits after the calm. If, however, the Borderline is the one who is inflicting the pain, they acquire a feeling of being in control. This is why the Borderline must abandon you; they have to do it before you can abandon them.

Chapter 2

My Early Years

Journal: *Always tired . . . lonely inside. Laughter is my only way out . . . or is it?*

Growing up, I was the youngest in our family of five. And oh, did I lap up being the baby of the family! If at any time there was no laughter, I decided there needed to be some. I would say something funny, sing something silly, or even act out something impromptu. I would do whatever it took to keep the family in stitches.

A Borderline craves attention and approval from everyone around them, and I was no exception. For instance, there were times when we came together as a family to practice a song we were going to sing at church. Right in the middle of a serious moment I would cut loose with a whole line of the song—opera style—and end with a belly laugh, hoping everyone would join in. But it didn't happen like that. Instead, there was Dad, looking over his glasses at me. It was the dreaded look that said, "I really mean business!"

> A Borderline craves attention and approval from everyone around them.

Dad never spanked me; he didn't have to. His look said it all. Then I had a problem. In my little mind I would interpret The Look as his way of saying, "I don't approve of you," and my heart would break. Dad probably had no clue I read his comments and looks that way. It was all inside me. Even at such a young age I had developed a coping mechanism that involved unhealthy thinking patterns. I'm sure Dad would get very frustrated with me, not knowing why I acted the way I did. He never really understood the reason why I broke up serious moments: it was my main outlet for the fear and anxiety.

Another symptom of unhealthy thinking was my reaction to my childhood nickname—Dough Brain, or sometimes Dodo Bird—used mainly by my siblings. Young children don't realize what they're setting in motion by their words. They're just being kids. I'm sure people who called me Dodo Bird had no clue how the nickname lodged in my mind. I took it to heart; I owned it; and it became a part of me. But Mom and Dad had no inkling what was going on inside my head and heart.

I suppose the practice of siblings acquiring innocent little names for each other is a common occurrence among young children, one that affects individuals in various ways. Unfortunately for some, a nickname has a far-reaching effect that causes problems later in life. For me, it was that I grew up feeling stupid. I can't recall a single time when I thought I could conquer something, or find the answer to something. It was always, "I can't do this." Although it's hard to believe, I came very close to flunking kindergarten.

Another complication was that I was being sexually abused. I'm sure it affected my performance at school. In first grade, after complaining of stomach pain to my mom and making numerous trips to the school nurse, Mom decided to have my stomach upsets checked out. The results revealed I was developing an ulcer. Mom and Dad never put it together that the ulcer was probably the result of my inner turmoil. As in most families, life was busy and there wasn't time to figure out every little thing.

Sometimes Mom would ask me to do a task, and if I didn't get it done to her satisfaction the first time, she would make me do it over. This would go on until she finally handed the job to my older sister. In my mind this only reinforced how stupid I was and that I couldn't do anything right. To be fair, Mom was probably thinking, *I will take the pressure off of Jodie, and her older sister can handle an additional task.* In reality, if I was told to do a job that had more than one step, I really struggled with processing the instruction. It was very frustrating and left me feeling helpless. But nobody knew what was going on inside my mind. I was unaware that I was setting myself up for failure.

I loved my dad very much and I believe he tried to be the best dad he could be. Unfortunately, all he had known since he was a little boy was a four-letter word: "work." He was thirteen when his mom passed away, and with eight children in the family, a heavy load of responsibility landed on his shoulders. It was a sad and rough time for a young teenager.

That same year his dad left to seek work elsewhere, leaving the kids to manage the household. My dad often talked about the hard times that year. He spoke of the hundreds of tomatoes he canned. He was responsible for putting dinner on the table every night. He worked in the garden and the fields. As a thirteen-year-old, his chores must have seemed endless. I can only imagine the heartbreak he must have felt during those important years of his life, and how much he missed the touch of his mother and the sound of her voice. At age eighteen my dad left home and joined the army.

Yes, my dad knew how to work—long, long hours. Not only did he work several jobs, he was always working on more than one project at any given time. There was hardly anything my dad could not do or build. He even started his own business, a tool and die shop. It was a great success.

Dad wasn't a touchy-feely kind of guy. He wasn't one to give hugs and kisses on the cheek. He expressed his love through provision. He was a tall, lanky man with a quick smile, but you had to be looking to catch that smile. As fast as it came, it was gone. I always enjoyed his unique, dry humor. Dad could say something so funny out of nowhere, and there was that quick smile. I don't ever remember Dad having a good ole belly laugh, though. Maybe he didn't know how to have a fun, carefree moment. He never got that chance growing up. But I'm sure he would have enjoyed it, because laughter is the best medicine.

As a little girl I don't remember ever receiving a reassuring hug or a love pat on the shoulder from my dad. There were no cozy sit-down chats or interesting conversations. Men who grew up in the same era as my sweet dad didn't know how to do these kinds of things. It was foreign to them. All they knew was to work and provide the shelter, food, and all the miscellaneous needs of a family.

I desperately needed my dad's attention, and I recall at least two different times that he gave it to me. One day, I was having a great time riding my bicycle up and down the driveway. As I often did, I tried to slow down by dragging my little toes on the ground, which, on this occasion, tore the skin off the tips of my toes. Dad scooped me up, carried me upstairs, placed me on a chair, and proceeded to cover the sore spots with iodine. Wow! Did it ever sting! But my little heart pounded with excitement that my dad, my knight in shining armor, had rescued me.

The other moment was when my siblings and I were in the basement of our house playing a game of "hot or cold." My brother had hidden an object that my sister and I were anxiously searching for. As we hunted he would call out, "You're getting cold . . . now hotter . . . hotter . . . hot!" We were almost there.

My sister and I realized the object must be up on the window sill, but we couldn't reach it. So I grabbed a chair and climbed aboard. My sister wanted to be the first one to find it, so she clambered aboard as well. Without warning, the chair tumbled over and I fell, hitting the back of my head on the concrete floor. I knew then what "seeing stars" meant. Dad heard me screaming, "I'm gonna die! I'm gonna die!" He rushed down the stairs and carried me back upstairs, reassuring me I would not die. Sitting me on his lap, he called our pastor to pray.

How I wish I could have told my dad what was really happening in my life. These were moments when I desperately needed his approval and assurance. Growing up, I would wonder if I was ever going to succeed at anything. But my dad was busy trying to make a living for our family. He had no idea I desperately needed the security of his attention. He wasn't aware of the things that were crushing me. If he had known, he could have rescued me once again from the things that would damage my life for many years. I wanted to tell him, but I chose to bottle it up inside. And nothing was ever the same again.

Only about 38 percent of child victims disclose the fact that they have been sexually molested. –J. J. Broman-Fulks, et al., *Journal of Clinical Child and Adolescent Psychology* (2007).

I struggled badly in school, but I never told my parents. I just lived and moved in my dark, secret world. At times my teachers tried to reach out to me, but I was too embarrassed to raise my hand or ask for help. I thought if they ever called on me, everyone would find out how stupid I was.

But there was one thing I could do that Dad took pride in. He had always loved music from the bottom of his soul; although he never took a lesson, he was proficient with the guitar, banjo, mandolin, bass, and dulcimer. He even crafted some of these instruments, and they were beautiful. Dad instilled his love of music in us kids. He wanted each one of us to learn to play an instrument. From time to time he would yell, "Kids, get your instruments! Let's play a tune or two!" Of course, it was always more than two. I think this was Dad's favorite connection with us kids. Of course, there was no laughing; this was serious business and everyone needed to hit the right notes and play well. Dad was a perfectionist. Everything must be done right and in perfect order.

As I mentioned, Dad took pride in my musical ability and thought I could play anything I wanted to. It was inevitable that I messed up many times while playing for church, and coming home I would be sad that I had made such a terrible mistake. Dad would say, "Aw, Jo, it wasn't that bad." Thank you, Dad, for that. I still remember those words, and every time I mess up I can hear my dad telling me, "Aw, Jo, it wasn't that bad."

Mother told me many years ago that as a toddler, I used to cry when Dad went off to work and would walk around in his house shoes for hours. He passed away on February 3, 2015, and the next morning I asked my mom, "Can I have Dad's house shoes?" She said yes, and I wore them around the house all that day. Wearing or holding something Dad had touched—his house shoes, his robe, his cane, his Bible—brought me the closeness I needed.

Mom grew up in a family of ten children. She had an alcoholic dad and a distant mom. They were very poor, and moved from place to place, sometimes camping under a tree in the truck. Mom's father had been gassed during the World War II and came back all messed up.

Mom related many horror stories from her childhood years. When she was about six, she contracted polio and was hospitalized for seven months. Her parents came to see her only two times during her hospital stay. When she finally came home, there were only two weeks left of the school term, and she refused to go back because she was so far behind everyone else. Her frustrated mother locked her in her bedroom, placing a bucket in her room for a toilet, saying, "You'll stay in there until the two weeks are up." For meals, her mother slid food under the bedroom door. I can only imagine what that kind of punishment would do to a child. That was one of many other abuses Mom experienced while growing up. Her elementary education ended at the sixth grade level.

Mom also came from the generation that believed in hard work. When she was still quite young, her father took her and the other siblings out to the potato fields so they could all earn money digging potatoes. Each child would then hand their earnings to their father. This was their way of life.

Mom was left with a great deal of scars from her past, but in her own way she wanted to be the best mom she could be while trying to work through areas that were tough for her. She didn't want us kids to have to live like she had. She wanted us to have a clean house and good food on the table. Because of this our house was always immaculate! We could find Mom mopping the floors late at night, as if she was wiping out the memory of living in houses with dirt floors. She would overdo at times and as a result was often sick.

Children need to feel safe and secure before they can trust adults. If the basic trust they need doesn't have a chance to develop, their personality cannot develop properly.

Healthy people who develop basic trust early in life can learn to accept responsibility for both their failures and successes. When parents or caregivers care for their children with empathy, support, and lots of patience, their children develop basic trust and the sense of comfort, security, and safety they need.

Most parents strive to be the best they can be, and most of them succeed. But it must be acknowledged that no kids have been raised perfectly, because we are all imperfect people. As the generations pass, patterns of discipline and behavior, either good or bad, are repeated over and over again. Consequently, many parents cannot cope because they don't really know the best way to handle a situation. All parents have experienced such moments, and sometimes when they look back, they wish they would have used different words, different actions, or another form of discipline.

I'm bringing this point out because we tend to look through rose-colored glasses at our childhood. Everyone has had wonderful times and good memories, along with some not so good. Others have only a few good memories, and I'm so sorry. But this is where we must all be honest with ourselves. We must look at the actions or decisions our parents made in raising us, both the bad and the good. This doesn't label them as bad people; it simply means they were trying to do the best they knew how in an imperfect world. Many times as we reflect on our childhoods, we can identify actions or words—or lack thereof—that affected us. It is needful that we do this because it is part of our story, part of what made us who we are. It's an underlying cause of how we process our thinking, how we look at life.

In order to survive I needed an atmosphere of fun, laughter, and happiness. This was my escape from the pain and hurt I carried around. On the other hand, silence made me very uncomfortable. I always associated silence with trouble, and it was very scary. It gave me a bad feeling to be around someone who was quiet or had little to say. Thus as a small child, I cannot remember ever being content with who I was. Instead, I began to develop the art of dissociation.

In simple terms, children in unendurable situations will dissociate—"space out"—by mentally traveling far from the present reality to another world, a happy world, a world they made all by themselves. When entering into the make-believe, they can now pretend they aren't really the person who is in pain. I learned dissociation at a very young age. As a youngster, I didn't understand what I was doing; I just knew it was a way to escape painful realities. I did a great deal of daydreaming.

Unfortunately, once learned, dissociation is very hard to break. You may have heard the expression, "The light's on but nobody's home." That was me. People would laughingly refer to me as "a blond." I know now that I wasn't a dumb blond; I was just a little girl in a dissociative state. People in a dissociative state are forgetful, scatterbrained, and unorganized. They appear to have nothing together; they have the look of helplessness.

My greatest fear was abandonment or losing my mama. She was often sick, and was hospitalized several times over the years. At one point she suffered a cardiac arrest during which her heart stopped beating for three minutes. This frightened me, and anytime she was sick in bed, I worried.

> Dissociation can be defined as disruptions in aspects of consciousness, identity, memory, physical actions, and/or the environment. When symptoms become severe, they can disrupt daily life.

Our family didn't sit around in the evening, resting, snacking, or engaging in small talk. Many evenings when I would be missed, Mom would find me already in bed for the night, sound asleep. I was always tired and needed extra hours of sleep to get through the next day. Pain was very exhausting. I needed a safe place and some solitude, a place where I didn't have to hear anything or think anything. I didn't feel as though I belonged; I felt disjointed. I pretended a lot. Life at times was like living a dream—sometimes even a nightmare. I didn't know it back then, but these are feelings children experience when they are coping with sexual abuse. They tell no one and suffer in silence.

I desperately wanted stability as a little girl, but I lived every day holding back the pain caused by a terrible secret. For me, life was a giant roller coaster rushing through twists and turns, throwing me upside down at times. It left me wondering when it all was going to end. I really didn't know who I was or what I was supposed to be.

Experiencing a traumatic event would churn up my insides faster than anything. Like the time we got a new puppy. I was so thrilled to have something to hold and cuddle. It made me feel loved. One evening the puppy and I were in the basement chasing each other around and around, and I was giggling, feeling almost content. But suddenly I realized it was time to go upstairs. I scooped up the wiggly puppy and hurried upstairs, thinking I had him in a firm grip. But to my dismay, I

> A person with Borderline Personality Disorder deals with internal struggles that consist of three major feelings: terrifying aloneness, feeling misunderstood, and overwhelming helplessness. They lack stability in every area of their life.

dropped him. He fell between the stairs and hit the basement floor with a thud. I was beside myself. What if he was badly hurt? The poor puppy ran around and around the basement yelping piteously at the top of his lungs. My heart cried out, *Oh, poor puppy, please don't cry*! I was devastated. My insides churned as I tried to process what I had just done. It turned out the puppy was fine, but it didn't take much to send me reeling inside.

My sister gave me a great deal of comfort during those stormy years. She was three and a half years older than I. We were close and got along very well. She would step up quite often and help Mom with chores and cooking at times when Mom was ill or hospitalized.

My sister was always very patient with me even though we were opposites. She was organized and scheduled; I wasn't.

Some of the happy times of my childhood were with my sister. We often slept together and would giggle and giggle. We had so much fun sneaking snacks into our room. One time my sister and I decided to put our allowance together and buy a giant-size bag of cheese curls. We were so excited! We took the bag to our room that night and—yes—we ate the whole bag, thinking Mom would never find out. We woke up so sick the next morning I'm sure Mom knew, but she never said.

My sister covered for me on more than one occasion. I was the sibling that would carelessly do something without heeding the outcome. She was the lighthouse in the middle of the storm. When the waves came rolling in I knew I could count on my sister.

I had one older brother. He was the quiet one, the only boy. We didn't hang together much more than playing Monopoly once in a while. Our Monopoly games could last for days. That was one of the fun times involving my brother that I remember the most.

From beginning to end, no matter how bad or how good, God knew every little thing about me. I was a work in progress. Philippians 1:6 says, "Being confident of this very thing, that He who has begun a good work in you will complete it until the day of Jesus Christ." That is a verse worth clinging to.

Chapter 3

Sexual Abuse

This You have seen, O LORD; do not keep silence. O Lord, do not be far from me. Stir up Yourself, and awake to my vindication, to my cause, my God, and my Lord. (Psalm 35:22–23)

Journal: *I'm lying in bed all alone. It's very quiet. Doors are locked and everyone is tucked in for a good night's sleep. But not me. I don't like being alone. I'm afraid of the dark. Bedtime is the worst time for me, for my mind and my spirit. In the dark all by myself my thoughts don't make sense. I would feel safe if I could be with someone, but I'm even afraid to walk to the restroom, much less another person's room. Someone or something might jump out and scare me. Nevertheless, great need causes me to get up and go anyway. Is it wrong? It has to be wrong. Oh, I'm so afraid. I need someone to help me!*

I was sexually abused from age four until age twelve. Thus for years and years I was always looking and thinking through the lens of sexual abuse. What is sexual abuse? It is any contact or interaction (visual, verbal, or psychological) between a child/adolescent and an adult when the child/adolescent is being used for sexual stimulation of the perpetrator or any other person.

It is very hard for the male population to come forward and admit they were molested, much less seek help or counseling for the problem. It affects everything about them. It takes away their masculinity. It affects their relationships severely. Most men will go to their grave with no one knowing they were ever sexually abused. When sexual abuse starts so young and continues,

> About one in seven girls and one in twenty-five boys will be sexually abused before they turn eighteen. This includes contact abuse only. –C. Townsend and A. A. Rheingold in "Estimating a child sexual abuse prevalence rate for practitioners" (2013), Darkness to Light, Charleston, SC

it's like being thrown into a terrible unknown world. And when you stumble back into your own world, you can only wonder and try to make sense of what just took place.

After it was over, I would walk slowly back to my room, emotions in turmoil, not really understanding or comprehending what just took place. I was numb to the world. Mom and Dad didn't know; my sister didn't know. My family was unaware of the darkness in my life. Should I tell someone? Or was it better to keep it all to myself?

As I grew older, the abuse continued. I couldn't figure out a way to say no. It was all I knew, and for lack of courage to tell anyone, I just kept following along. It had become part of my routine, but there was so much fear, anxiety, and insecurity involved. It was like being weightless and having no choice as to what happened to me or what someone did to me. I felt isolated from everyone else and lived in my own make-believe world where everything moved at a fast pace out of control. Would it ever stop?

According to *The Wounded Heart* by Dr. Dan B. Allender, "there is data indicating that abuse victims forget or repress memories. Blocking memories at any age comes from pain, confusion, horror, shame, and sorrow, but it's possible for conscious suppression to move into distortion or even illusion. If it becomes illusion, the memory of one's past abuse can be totally blocked, wiped completely away."

I believe many people have reached this state of repression. They don't remember the painful things that took place in their childhood. They believe the recollection of those memories would be the death of them, but this belief is a lie from Satan. Remembering these things is a truth that will set them free!

As I look back at those years long ago, I can see that I blocked out much of the abuse that was happening. I did not realize as a little girl that I was participating in sexual abuse. It had drawn me into a tiny, cramped world where I didn't know anyone. It's almost as if I wasn't living; I was just existing in a world that was standing still.

Sexual abuse is confusing for a small child. It messes up the process of maturation of the brain. It distorts a child's reasoning, and their skewed way of processing things will haunt and confuse them the rest of their life.

I don't think anyone likes to admit such a thing happened to them. There is too much shame involved, and it's too painful to talk about. It's easier to say, "I was taken advantage of" or "I was involved in something that made me feel uncomfortable" or "I did something I didn't want to do." But when you open up and acknowledge that you were sexually abused, it's like you have just opened a can of worms and can't get the lid back on. If you do manage to force the lid back down, the "can" becomes a pressure cooker of emotion and in time you will explode.

Trusting people will open their souls to others and hope they won't take advantage of their vulnerability. Children are supposed to learn about trusting and loving in the very early years of their life. But my life had been tainted with so much dysfunction and sexual abuse, there was no way I could learn a healthy way to trust and love.

The victim's struggle to trust will be proportionately related to the extent of their parents' failure to protect and nurture them as a child. This statement speaks volumes! It took

> As many as 40 percent of children who are sexually abused are abused by older, or more powerful children. –D. Finkelhor (2012), "Characteristics of crimes against juveniles," Durham, NH: Crimes Against Children Research Center.

many years for me to understand this—until I was in my forties.

We sometimes blame our parents or another family member for not protecting us and making sure we were okay. But we must look deep into our soul and spirit and examine this for ourselves. I don't think any parent, relative, or family member would approve of their little one being sexually abused. Truth is, most of the time they don't have a clue it is happening. Their neglect of the problem is totally unintentional. But even if the neglect was unintentional, we must still forgive and let it go.

When children are sexually abused, in their mind it involves the whole family, whether or not they know it. Children have only partial understanding. They watch their family members and how they respond. They notice facial expressions and the tone of voice. Those reflections determine not only who the children are, but what they will become. Over time all of these reflections become part of the children, and they take on the shape of the person they see in the family looking glass.

Think back to your young childhood and remember how you felt when you were instructed to do something. How did the person sound? Gentle or gruff? Did their tone leave you with a positive feeling of "I can do this?" Or did you detect a hint of negativity in their voice? You were either left with the let-down feeling "They don't think I can do this" or with the empowering feeling "They think I can do this!"

No matter how soft, gentle, and caring a parent may sound, their body language can say something quite different. When this occurs, their body language becomes about 90 percent of what they are conveying. It can be the great eye roll, a scowl, an irritated grimace, or a distant stare indicating, "I'm not connecting with you. I'm busy."

Because of the abuse, I know my communication skills were off from the very beginning, and my view of love was totally messed up. I struggled for many years with the belief that love was just an emotion. It wasn't about words or relationship; it was all about the body—if someone liked your body, then they loved you. When it came to pleasing someone or getting their approval, I thought it was all about the body. I was off to a very bad start.

For many people, shame is another word for embarrassment. Everyone has experienced horrible embarrassment at some time or another. And they can still remember, as if it were yesterday, what it felt like to be humiliated in front of a group of people. Just thinking about it makes them cringe. There are places they won't revisit and people they won't hang around with because of embarrassment. They don't intend to allow themselves to be in that position ever again!

However, shame is not the same as embarrassment; it's a counterpart to embarrassment. Shame is a silent killer. It can slowly kill our hearts, our goals, everything we thought we were and everything we were meant to be. Shame stops us dead in our tracks. It can keep us from ever excelling in anything.

Nobody wants to admit, "I was sexually abused." That would be like exposing oneself in public. No one wants to experience that feeling of deep shame. They avoid telling anyone for fear of rejection, which would make matters much worse!

29

Then there is always that dreaded moment of silence after you've had the courage to say, "I was sexually abused." If the person to whom you said it has also been sexually abused, they are feeling and thinking those thoughts all over again. They may have vowed no one would ever know they were sexually abused, but when they hear it from you, the abuse suddenly rises to stare at them like an ugly monster. They try desperately not to let it show on their face, but they feel as if you can see right through them.

I have found that as you reveal how God has helped you recover from a life of abuse that you can sense the atmosphere, and sometime you are setting the stage for someone to say something they've needed to say for a long time but were afraid to do so. These are God moments that can start people on the path to freedom.

John 8:32 states, "And you shall know the truth, and the truth shall make you free." We must be true to ourselves. No more sugar-coating or beating around the bush. Just as an alcoholic must first admit, "I am an alcoholic!" in order to get on the road to recovery, we must also admit what happened to us.

Sexually abused people often feel marked for life, as if they could never walk far enough away to avoid the issue. This will remain true as long as the problem is not dealt with. Yes, the abuse will always be part of our life story, but God can take what was meant for evil and work it for our good! "And we know that all things work together for good to them that love God, to them who are the called according to His purpose" (Romans 8:28).

God will allow situations and circumstances in our lives in order to help us on our journey to our heavenly home. Life sometimes seems to throw curveballs our way, but God will take those events and make them come out for our good—that is, if we allow Him to. We want only good things to happen to us, but that isn't life. Everyone around us has a different story to tell, and each one reacts differently to the circumstances and events in their lives. Some allow God to heal and restore them, while others become bitter and stay in a life of defeat. God is not looking to help us feel comfortable on earth; He is preparing our way and helping us to grow, heal, and be restored.

II Corinthians 12:9 states, "And He said to me, 'My grace is sufficient for you, for My strength is made perfect in weakness.'" In your weakness He is made strong!

Chapter 4

The Internal Impact of Sexual Abuse

Journal: *Why does life have to be like this? I know I'm eventually going to make it, but right now I don't think I can.*

Caught up in the minutiae of everyday life, we don't realize that every action we take and every decision we make impacts our family roles and how they play out. Children can easily become confused about what to do and whom to listen to for instruction. It's important to make sure the family is following the biblical guidelines on how we are to operate on a daily basis. Not every family is perfect, but all families should strive to be Christlike in everything.

There are absolutely no words to describe what sexual abuse does to an innocent child. It strips away all the God-given emotions and responses. It dirties up the mind, and the thinking process is rerouted to an unhealthy thinking pattern. Looking through the lens of the tainted soul is like looking through fake glass; it is so distorted that there is no sense to be made of it.

> Sexual abuse is like a silent killer; it wrecks the heart, soul, and mind.

I had no idea what sexual abuse could do or how it would affect every aspect of my life, relationships, goals, and, most important, my personal walk with God. But I can't go back and do anything over; what's done is done, and I'm left with the only possible solution: to somehow learn to deal with the blows that the sexual molestation caused in my life.

Sexual abuse is like a silent killer; it wrecks the heart, soul, and mind. It first of all strips away the meaning of what God intended the family to be. Anytime a child is sexually abused, it strips away the child's innocence and the effects are seen within the family. The devil hates anything that God created, especially our families, the first human institution God created. Families are very important to God!

The love between a man and a woman represents the love between Christ and the church.

Ephesians 5:25 says, "Husbands, love your wives, just as Christ also loved the church and gave himself for her." The devil would love nothing better than to tear down the institution of marriage that God created for us to live by. If there is a breakdown between Mom and Dad it will always trickle down to the children. The best thing a man can do for his children is to love his wife.

There is dysfunction in every family to a certain degree. We are all imperfect people trying to do our best. In our everyday struggle to teach, manage, and juggle all the aspects of family life, we don't realize how many of our decisions and actions are unhealthy. We are merely doing what we think is right at the time. We are carrying the baggage we have picked up along the way, which sometimes includes incorrect ways our parents learned how to handle things.

I was always afraid of the dark—I mean *really* afraid. I feel as though this was directly related to the abuse because most of the sexual abuse occurred at nighttime. I can still remember a night long ago around the age of seven. My brother was away for the night and I was sleeping in his bed. My brother always liked big stuffed animals in his room. I woke up in the middle of the night and turned over. There on the nightstand was a very large, dark shape staring at me. I let out a horrific scream and ran out of the room. I was terrified. My mom and dad tried to get me back in bed, but I could not, would not, enter that room. I don't even know what my thoughts were that dreadful night. I just remember the horrible fear I had and how gut-wrenching it was.

I have many unpleasant memories of being afraid at night. I can remember lying awake for hours, my heart pounding, thinking I was seeing scary things. Being afraid of the dark carried on into my adult life. I can remember sleeping with the lights on many nights when my husband had to be gone on preaching trips or other things. It's one of those things I was embarrassed about. What grown woman wants to tell anyone she's afraid of the dark?

Sexual abuse, in its own cruel way, almost seems okay. Once done, it can never be retracted. One can never go back and say, "I wasn't molested." The hearts of people who have suffered a heart attack will never be the same again. They will always have a defective heart to a certain degree. Yes, they can go on to live a productive life, but they can't do everything they used to. They will have to change their activities and their diet. They have to change in order to succeed. The same is true with sexual abuse. In order to succeed in life, you must at some point get the help you need in order to get through the healing process.

There are two types of sexual abuse: *contact* and *interaction.* Contact varies from most severe to least severe and involves anything from manual touching of body parts through clothes to full body contact through intercourse. No matter the extent of the abuse, the child will still suffer. Abuse within the family will have lasting negative effects.

Interactions, as seen in the list below, also can happen within in a broad spectrum.

- Verbal: sexual names as personal names; the repeated use of sexual language
- Visual: exposure to pornography, inappropriate attention to sexual organs
- Psychological: The use of a child for a surrogate spouse; sexual/physical boundary violation

Even if the sexual abuse is subtle, it is still just as damaging. I believe there are adults who have been sexually abused in such a subtle way that they don't even realize it. They are suffering and have untold grief in their life and their families, but they have come up with no answers. I want to encourage you by saying if you are reading this book, and you're suffering with no apparent way out, there is hope for you.

For a child, the most soul-damaging type of abuse is by a family member. It disrupts and distorts the relationships within the family, leaving the child with no one to turn to for help. To the child of incest, there is no such thing as a safe home. Instead, their safe haven becomes their church, school, or even a trusted friend's home. Unfortunately, the dysfunction continues to destroy everything in its path. Later in life, sexual abuse can lead victims into broken relationships, loneliness, depression, eating disorders, promiscuity, sexual coldness, and uncontrollable rage.

I had my share of broken relationships. My first marriage ended in divorce after ten years of marriage and four little boys. I was devastated. My first husband left me for another woman—not just another woman, but a married woman with three children. That first marriage was unhealthy from the beginning. I was very young. I had a great deal of pain and heartache, and, although I didn't know it, I was already suffering from the symptoms of BPD. I really had no idea how to truly love someone. You cannot love someone else until you love and accept yourself. Who is the hardest person to get along with? The person who doesn't like himself.

As long as I can remember, I have felt very lonely. No one ever knew, though, because I covered it up well. I spent a great deal of time being dissociated, existing in my own world of dreams, imagination, and make-believe. This was, I think, my number-one way of coping with the abuse.

Because of the sexual abuse, I lacked proper boundaries in my dating relationships. I was allowed to start dating around the age of twelve, and I made many wrong choices in whom to date. If your view of yourself is an unhealthy one, you lose your identity and who you really are. You allow people to say things and do things against you because you think you deserve it. There is no self-respect. All dignity is lost. As for me, all I can do is look back and thank God for His hand of mercy upon my life.

> Who is the hardest person to get along with? The person who doesn't like himself.

I grew up with a great deal of anger, but I was an expert in masking it with laughter. In fact, I kept my anger bottled up so well that as a first grader I experienced a great deal of stomach pain and nausea. My mom, ignorant about the sexual abuse, received a call from the school nurse, who informed her I was coming to see her quite often. The nurse recommended that my mom take me to the doctor for an evaluation.

Upon the completion of X-rays and additional tests, they found I had the beginnings of an ulcer. Shocked, Mom told the doctor, "But she's the clown of the family, always laughing and very entertaining!" The doctor replied, "Those are the types of kids that suffer inside. They cover their pain up that way." Still, I never told my mom about the ongoing sexual abuse in my life. I never even hinted there was anything unpleasant going on.

During this time I also started wetting the bed, another sign of a child being sexually abused. My mother constantly worked with me over the bed-wetting issue.

Sexual abuse strips away the freedom to choose. The abuse is not by choice, so therefore you feel as though you are utterly powerless. You don't have choices. Things and events just happen to you. They catch you off guard and it causes you to think, *I'm just a small wave in the middle of the ocean, not knowing where I will end up.*

You have this urge, a longing for people to think everything is great and wonderful in your life. You want them to think you have it all together, that you are happy all the time.

Pain is a gift, but we never welcome it. Pain just barges through the front door like an intruder. None of us like pain, so we do what we have to do in order to avoid it or cover it up through dissociation.

Many years ago a doctor found in his studies while treating people with leprosy that the disease destroyed them through the loss of feeling in their nerve endings. The lack of "protective pain" made them

> Pain is a gift, but we never welcome it. Pain just barges through the front door like an intruder.

vulnerable to burns, cuts, exposure to destructive pressure to the hands and feet, untended wounds, and infection. This invisible disability made them unable to tell if they were in a dangerous situation. That's why I say pain is a gift. The absence of it can prove fatal.

This is an apt parallel to those of us who have covered up our pain; we literally kill our souls. We deaden or numb our souls to avoid feeling pain. When we dissociate ourselves from pain, we lose our sense of being alive. We are dead through and through! Everyone struggles through ups and downs and unfortunate circumstances, but for those who have suffered from sexual abuse, it's twice as hard to function and navigate through it all.

Shame is a horrible thing. It's like a slow bleed. Have you ever been around someone with a slow bleed? You start noticing little by little something is wrong but you can never put your finger on it. At times they have trouble with their speech or processing a simple daily task. But as quickly as it comes, it goes, and suddenly you think, *Was I seeing things? They seem to be okay now.*

Shame makes you view the world through a clouded lens. You feel different, as if the words were written all over your face, and you think people are looking down on you. They must know everything—the whole story. Every failure, every loss you experience is just another reminder of your past. Shame is an enemy that tears to shreds the innermost parts of your soul. Dr. Dan B. Allender, in his book *The Wounded Heart*, indicates that shame has three elements.

> *(1) Exposure*: Exposure requires another person, whether in reality or in imagination, for its blow to be felt. Our dark secret has been found out! Sexually abused people will at times feel marked for life, as though the abuse has set them apart from the "normal" people. They feel they will never be the same again.
>
> *(2) Revelation*: We think people can see the deficiency in our dignity. We are somehow and forever brought down to a lower place, a place for people who are no longer whole anymore.
>
> *(3) Consequences*: Another element in shame is the anticipated outcome when people know the truth of what happened in your life. There's a terrible fear of rejection. What will happen if your secret is discovered? Will you ever be wanted again?

I remember the first time I acknowledged I had been sexually abused. It was terribly uncomfortable; I greatly feared rejection or being looked on as dirty. But at the same time my admission was freeing; I had let it out and it was no longer a dark, shameful secret. It's the secret that will eat you alive if it's not brought to light and taken care of.

In reality, when we are ready to tell someone about our sexual abuse, it's usually a close family member or friend, depending on our age at the time. It usually is not planned; it suddenly slips out of our mouth because it has been on the tip of our tongue for some time. We have wanted people to know, but we couldn't figure out how or when to reveal it. I have found that most of the time, when someone is told, they respond with empathy, concern, and care. If, however, their response is the opposite, they too may have some grave issues stirring below the surface of their life.

Sexual abuse robs you of the ability to trust. Going through life without trusting anyone is painful. It disrupts all of your relationships. Without trust, there is no complete or healthy relationship. You live life as a victim with a victim mentality, always suspicious of the motives of others. Every relationship is marred by an invisible wall that divides you from them. You feel you must protect yourself against everyone because at any given time you could feel that pain all over again through rejection or abandonment.

Worst of all, your trust in God is damaged. Your trust must start with God, and then work its way down though all of your others relationships. Without trust, your life is shallow and incomplete. It's impossible to grow in God without first trusting Him.

The average Christian has difficulty developing trust in their walk with God. When sexual abuse is added to that, the matter of trust suddenly hits a brick wall. Now you must chisel away at the wall a little at a time. Granted, that is hard work but it can be done. Nothing is impossible with God!

Philippians 4:13 states, "I can do all things through Christ who strengthens me." This verse has become permanently lodged in my inner core of thought. I have relied upon this verse to get me through many tough times.

Ambivalence is perhaps one of the most damaging elements of sexual abuse. It means having two contradictory emotions at the same time. This is such a devastating feeling! It messes with your judgment between right and wrong. It compounds the shame you feel by piling on mass confusion.

I did not realize until many years later that ambivalence in itself is abuse. A young child thinks that if it doesn't hurt and it feels good, it must be okay. I was so young when the abuse started that I didn't realize the harm in it. Later, as I owned and accepted the fact that I had been

> For a child, sexual abuse, even multiple episodes, is not seen as terrifying or life threatening at the time. –William Cromie (2006), *The Harvard Gazette*

sexually abused, it caused a great deal of shame for me knowing that as a little girl I felt comfort during those times. It was indeed a good feeling. Can you see how confusing this was?

Sexual pleasure is both frightening and pleasantly stimulating to a young child. It feels like something warm and fuzzy has been added to your empty heart. But this same pleasure comes with a high price. Somewhere in the dark recesses of the mind you realize you are being horribly violated. It is betrayal of the worst kind, and the amount of damage that happens to a child is untold.

I probably will never remember some of my thoughts and feelings during those years, but I did harbor a tremendous amount of anxiety. It's like being betrayed by your own body. You think, *If it's wrong, why does it bring pleasure?* You also feel as though you are responsible for what's happening, especially if the abuser has your cooperation.

I've always felt that a portion of my mind was out of my control. I constantly dwelt on what was happening and began to view myself as a toy rather than an intelligent human being. I saw myself as dirty and cheap. I didn't deserve being treated like a person of value and strength. All of this was, of course, part of the victim mentality. It kept me from achieving in every area of life. I also viewed everyone else through the same lens; I didn't place any value on anybody else in my circle.

Victims of sexual abuse do not respect and honor people because they don't know how. They feel as though their bodies are the criteria others judge them by. They become obsessed with what their bodies looks like. Appearance becomes their only concern. It's the only thing about them that has value.

Chapter 5

Secondary Symptoms of Sexual Abuse

Journal: *I'm out of sorts today. How do people see me? How can they understand me? They don't even know who I am . . .*

Sexual abuse not only destroys a victim's internal world, but also his or her external world. Like a festering splinter, whatever has been damaged and twisted on the inside will eventually work its way out.

I did not know to what extent I had been damaged, and I had lived that way for so long, the abuse now defined me. I didn't know what "normal" was. I guess I thought the way I was living and thinking was normal. When there is a great deal of dysfunction, and you live in it every day, this is your normal.

Most abused people you meet and talk to will deny that their experiences affected them deeply. Most people really don't see it. Some of it is denial and some of it is pride. Those who have been abused don't know how to be honest and upfront because they have lived their whole lives covering up the truth. Who really wants to admit they are messed up?

John 8:32 states, "And you shall know the truth, and the truth shall make you free."

The truth is the only thing that will totally set you free! I'm amazed that the very thing that will set us free is the thing we run away from. Have you ever seen or heard someone trying to save a drowning person, but the person is fighting them with everything they've got? They are fighting against their only means of getting safely to shore. In like manner, Borderlines fight the very person who is trying to help or save them.

The outward damage done by sexual abuse will show up in two ways: (1) secondary symptoms (depression, sexual dysfunction, etc.); (2) the

> The outward damage done by sexual abuse will show up in two ways: (1) secondary symptoms (depression, sexual dysfunction, etc.); (2) the abused person's style of relating to others.

40

abused person's style of relating to others. For years I exhibited these symptoms. I suffered from depression as long as I can remember—that is, until my healing. Depression is a horrible thing. In many cases, a person will go to a therapist not because of their sexual abuse, but because of depression, not realizing their depression is merely a symptom of something far more troubling.

The depression I suffered would become more prevalent during the down times in my life. As a little girl, I appeared to be an upbeat, happy-go-lucky girl that loved life and everything that went with it. This behavior continued on through my adult years. No one ever knew I was depressed because I covered it up so well. I spent far too many hours in my imaginary world, escaping the pain and anger that resided in me.

I hated school, starting with kindergarten, which I almost flunked. When I think back, I can't recall any good memories about school. It was a severe struggle and burden, and depression hindered me from even caring. I dreamed of being someone other than myself. I wished I was older. Maybe being older would bring some control into my life. I was never satisfied with where I was. I cannot remember studying for any kind of test or assignment. Instead, I did a lot of sleeping in school. I was always so tired, I couldn't think or even concentrate. My processing was slow. My mind was so messed up that it affected my learning ability. I wasn't required to show my parents my report cards, so they had no idea that I flunked a few classes. No matter; I was passed through to the upper grades anyway. However, a few days before graduation my teacher called me in and said I was not going to graduate unless I got caught up with a few assignments I had left undone. So I returned to school until I had enough credits to graduate. I had numerous nightmares for years after that. I would wake up in a cold sweat dreaming I was not going to graduate and would have to return to school for another semester.

My dream had always been to be a registered nurse and to marry a minister. I didn't accomplish either one. Instead, shortly before graduation I married my first husband, a computer programmer, and shortly after graduation I attended six weeks

> I had nightmares for years. I would wake up in a cold sweat.

of classes to become a CNA (Certified Nursing Assistant). Although it was nowhere near my dream, this small accomplishment was exciting. Unfortunately, my energy level and motivation always seemed at a low ebb, and I would come home after a day's work, fall into bed, and not wake up until it was time for work the next day. Depression made it almost impossible to hold down a full-time job along with taking care of a home. It was clearly too much for my damaged system.

I was so excited when I got pregnant with my first son! I had always wanted six children—and that was one dream I did accomplish! Jared was born June 26, 1981. But soon I was struggling to keep up with the intense amount of time and care a baby takes. I was barely managing to get things done. Fourteen weeks after Jared was born, I had a follow-up appointment and found that I was five weeks pregnant with baby number two. I broke down and cried. How was I going to cope with two babies only eleven months apart? Josh was born with a bad case of colic. I think I cried as much as he did!

Depression pushed me way down during this time. I was by myself a lot, and felt unbearably lonely. I was literally helpless and hopeless. I let my house go because tending two babies completely sapped my energy. My marriage was falling apart and I didn't know what to do. Victims of sexual abuse live with the fact that they had no choice then, and they have no choice now. When problems arise, they feel totally helpless. They somehow hope they can make it through with everything intact when it's all over.

When Jared and Josh were one and two, my husband left me for a few months, which set my mind to reeling. I had no job and no income. The only solution seemed to be moving back in with Mom and Dad. I don't know why my husband left, but he did come back, and it wasn't long until I was pregnant with baby number three, Dustin. Our marriage seemed to thrive for a short time, but after baby number four, Jordan, was born, the marriage fell apart once again, leaving me feeling helpless and out of control. I really counted on the tremendous amount of help I received from my parents. I don't

> I was determined that if I accomplished only one thing in life, it would be to take my boys to church.

know what I would have done without them. They helped me with the day-to-day care of my babies. They covered everything I needed financially. Those were some really tough years. When I look back on them, I wonder how I ever made it.

I did know one thing for sure: I loved my little boys with all my heart and tried my best to raise them right. Church was my refuge from the storm that raged inside my head. Unfortunately, I spent most church nights in the nursery with a crying baby. My husband had quit attending church when my second son was three months old. This left a huge hole in the circle of life. Going to church night after night with four young sons was almost more than I could handle, but I was determined that if I accomplished only one thing in life, it would be to take my boys to church and teach them how to love and live for God. I remember many trips to church when I had to pull over on the side of the road to get my little boys settled down. Sometimes I would think, *I just can't do this anymore*! But as the next church service rolled around, I found myself on the road to church once again.

During those early years I would lie in bed for hours, unable to sleep and crying my eyes out. My only comfort was to go to that imaginary world where everything was okay. I remember standing in the kitchen late one night holding a butcher knife in my hand, thinking, *What would it be like to just be gone? No more worries, no more depression, no more tears, no more pain . . .* I attempted to move on, but depression dogged my every step.

For those who are going through divorce, I have a valuable piece of advice: It is very important to get some professional counseling. If I had benefitted from professional counseling at that time, I might have recognized the damage that life had done to me and received the diagnosis and therapy I needed early on. But I continued to wallow in a slough of depression and a failed marriage, feeling hopeless and all alone. Many people think they would benefit most from moving on with their life into a new relationship. They are happy for a short period of time, but soon their problems and issues resurface, setting the cycle in motion all over again. Sadly, they don't realize they have dragged all their former baggage into the second relationship.

Secondary Symptoms

Depression: Depression comes in many forms. Depressed people often have insomnia. Or they might be the ones who never sit still. They stay busy doing one thing or another to occupy their mind and keep their inner thoughts at bay. Some workaholics are very depressed.

Depression is often referred to as "learned helplessness." I found this to be true. When everything else fails, the only thing to do is become depressed. Have you ever noticed how much attention someone gets when they're depressed? This attention-getting ploy sometimes gives the depressed person an adrenaline rush. I believe depression is the friend of just about everyone at one time or another. We all experience defeat, illness, or failure at different times throughout our lives.

Depression in people with Borderline Personality Disorder is a vicious cycle. They are depressed just about nonstop. Their depression pushes them way down, although it does have its peaks. Then they feel depressed because they're depressed. It's the worst kind of paradox. It's a hamster running on a wheel with nowhere to get off. The cycle has no end.

As stated above, most people will seek help for their depression, not for its underlying cause. Why? Number one, many people don't realize there is a correlation between depression and sexual abuse. Number two, the memory of the abuse has been blocked to the point there is no recall. Number three, depression may not set in until several years after the abuse occurred. But in the midst of counseling, many times the sexual abuse will surface, more so in females than in males.

Depressed people believe lies, and it feeds their depression. The following list of lies could go on and on:

1. People don't care about me.
2. God doesn't care about me.
3. I am all alone.
4. I am a failure.
5. I will never get better.
6. There is no use to even try.
7. Nobody loves me.

A depressed person thinks negatively. This is a dangerous place for you to be because it gives the devil an inroad into your thoughts, and you tend to believe every negative thing he feeds you, whether it's true or not!

Sexual Dysfunction and Addiction: Sexual dysfunction is a common outgrowth of sexual abuse. Many do not have severe issues with it, but memory takes them back to the place where the abuse happened, so there is going to be an effect. Sometimes it manifests in a sense of emptiness, a lack of intimacy, or a lack of interest. An abused person doesn't know how to open their whole heart because it's been buried under layers of scar tissue.

BPD usually triggers an addiction. Thankfully, this is one symptom I did not have. But I have watched many people suffering with addictions, and it is very painful. Addictions come in various forms: drugs, alcohol, sexual addictions, and the list goes on.

Many times someone who has been sexually abused will have a sexual addiction. Many men will struggle with sexual perversion. It's another reason why anger builds up in their mind and spirit.

Physical complaints: Are you always complaining about every ache and pain? I will acknowledge that physical illnesses can cause pain in people who were not sexually abused. On the other hand, some bodily pain is the result of abuse. Our bodies were never intended to be at war with our psyche. When we develop chronic headaches, low backaches, ulcers, stiff necks, tight jaws, and intestinal problems, it is our body screaming for help. Depression causes pain. People who become addicted to prescription drugs will actually have body pain and feel they need medication. If one can be freed of the abuse, the mind and spirit can heal, and the body aches and pains will improve or totally disappear.

Style of relating: Symptoms of sexual abuse are not always immediately present, but they will inevitably show up in our style of relating to others. Relational style can be described as the way we typically protect ourselves while in the presence of another person. We will do anything to avoid being hurt, powerless, or betrayed.

Relationships are where we are most likely to be hurt. A healthy relationship requires deep love, commitment, and honesty, but for an abuse victim those three things must be dodged at all cost. In the remainder of this chapter we will discuss three styles of relating suggested by Dr. Dan Allender in *The Wounded Heart: Hope for Adult Victims of Childhood Abuse.*

The Good Girl: The Good Girl is one who is willing to give all she has for the sake of peace, no matter what the cost. She is the classic helper and is very kindhearted. This girl appears to be home, but the lights aren't on. She's pleasant to talk to but is dead inside. Her soul is disengaged from most feelings except for guilt. Good girls feel as if they don't have a voice. It's very hard for them to speak up, and when they don't, they get frustrated with themselves. The internal world of a good girl is filled with self-contempt. She is lonely, passive, and controlled.

Externally, Good Girl is pleasant and sacrificial. She is an energetic worker, stays organized, performs well, and avoids asking for help; she would rather ignore her mental health than impose on anyone else. Good Girl is a martyr; she gives to others but does not invite them into her life or soul. She will not rest until she thinks everyone is pleased with her. She is one who continuously apologizes.

The Tough Girl: Tough Girl loves to take charge and has zero tolerance for nonsense. She appears to have a heart of gold, and she does—her heart is as hard as gold. This woman lives behind very thick, impregnable walls. Determined never to be hurt again, she detaches from her own feelings, and thus becomes suspicious of others' motives and intolerant of their emotional outbursts. She thinks it's childish to ask for help. Longing is a sign of weakness. She refuses to depend on anyone. She is arrogant and has very little interest in other people's thoughts or feelings. Tough Girl will either flare up in an instant or hold a grudge for a very long time. She is a lonely woman.

Externally, Tough Girl has a haughty stare, one that says, "I do not like you" or "Do not look at me." Tough Girl will be the one in charge. She's great at research and knows where to find the best bargains for everything. She will never admit to being wrong; she would rather drink poison and make everyone else pay for it. She will not accept compliments. She has a tough exterior and will not let anything sink into her spirit or soul.

46

The Party Girl: This girl is easygoing. Although she can be uptight at times, most often she is low key and calm. You can count on her—for being inconsistent, that is. She has the ability to easily pull you into her circle, but before you know it she can turn her back on you and leave you behind in the dust. Party Girl can come across as inviting and warm, but it turns out she's a whiney baby.

Internally, Party Girl is a paradoxical masterpiece; she's fragile but funny, sincere but phony, blunt but dishonest. She can be inconsistent and happy one minute, and full of doom and gloom the next. Her emotions are all over the chart with no rhyme or reason. A party girl will drive people crazy because they never know what to expect from her. She has strong feelings but has learned never to face them or let them go deep within her. She won't allow herself to feel too much because that would require honesty, and she just won't go there. It's much easier to cry or laugh over her pain and then walk away.

Externally, Party Girl will bounce around from relationship to relationship with no commitment or loyalty. The minute there is no more pleasure to be wrung out of the relationship, she leaves it behind and moves on to another.

> It is important that you open up your heart, spirit, and soul in order to see the real you.

She enters relationships to gratify her needs and self-satisfaction. She is far more interested in her needs being met than giving loyalty, honesty, and commitment to someone. If you let her down, she will look and act as though you totally failed and load you down with guilt. She prefers to be the center of attention. She is superficial and has no substance underneath.

I believe I was a party girl. I never could face reality and honesty. I laughed and cried my way through life.

Note: If you are suffering from past sexual abuse, I hope and pray this section will help you recognize your relational style. If you say, "But I can't figure out which one I am," just ask your spouse, parent, or close friend. It's hard sometimes to be honest with yourself and see who you really are and how you act. I guarantee that someone close to you will recognize your relational style. Next, it is important that you open up your heart, spirit, and soul in order to see the real you and how people view you. Accomplishing this will

help you as you read through the following chapters. Then you can
begin the healing process.

Chapter 6

My Teenage Years

Journal: *I'm the party girl. My insides are screaming, "Love me for what you see!"*

Children who have been sexually abused enter their preteen years totally unprepared. Their psychological immaturity pulls them into a cycle of failure and frustration. Their mistrust, low self-esteem, and lack of goals haunt their very being at every turn.

I cringe when I recall this time in my life; I get a sick feeling deep down within me when I realize just how poorly I was navigating. These are important years, years in which children should be setting goals and meeting challenges in order to reach the place where they want to be as they enter adulthood. This is difficult enough for the typical teenager. For one that has already accumulated a great amount of harmful baggage, it is almost impossible! Such a child desperately needs help and counseling.

My secret desire had always been to marry a minister; for me it was a calling to a higher place. Had I revealed this desire to someone in leadership, I could have been led in the right direction. A minister or pastor would have seen the calling in my life. Thankfully, at the age of thirty, after many twists and turns, I married the man of my dreams—a minister.

As a teenager, I loved God; He was my strength. I dearly loved the church and still do! Church was my life. I lived and breathed church. I can even remember crying if we had to miss church on occasion.

I never wanted to make wrong choices when it came to church standards. I loved creating the big hairdos, spending hours on my own as well as other people's hair. I have no idea how much hairspray I inhaled during those years. At youth camp my sister and I were the designated hairdressers. Most of the girls from our church didn't know how to fix their hair, so we volunteered. I don't ever remember missing a camp. I went to all of them. Good ole Westphalia!

I loved to worship—did I ever love to worship! I was very expressive in my praise to God. Most of the time you could find me on the front row at church. I wanted to be in the big middle of what God was doing. I taught Sunday school at a young age and loved it. In class I would have as many as thirty children around ages four or five. I loved to talk, so I'm sure this helped me with my ninety-thousand-word quota per day, with gusts up to a hundred thousand! I loved Sunday mornings and relished all the love, laughter, and joy those kids brought into my life.

During our teenage years my sister and I acquired the nursing home ministry. Along with our youth pastor, we would visit nursing home residents twice every weekend, rarely missing a service. We had such a great time! One stop was right after Sunday school every Sunday. The facility was located in an old house. I would drag my accordion up two flights of stairs and play and sing while those elderly people joined in, their faces coming alive as we sang. At times the stench from some of those rooms would be almost unbearable, but still, I wouldn't miss the opportunity for anything.

The nursing home we visited every Saturday was a bit nicer. I didn't need to lug my accordion along because they had a piano in the dining room. They would bring all the elders there when we arrived for service. It was amazing to watch them worship God together. They would sob as we held their hands. For many of them, we were the only visitors they had. These are precious memories I wouldn't trade for anything.

I believe the thing that held me together, other than my love for God, was my love for music. My parents could find me playing the piano at any given hour of the day. Sometimes after coming home from church I would sit down at the piano and try to figure out what I had heard someone play that night at church. I had a great desire to develop the talent God had given me. It was soothing to sit down and play from my heart and soul. I started playing the piano for youth service at age twelve. I loved it! From this point on, I always played for church, and as the years passed, I covered the Sunday services as well.

I had mentors that helped me tremendously. They were my great inspired pastors! I remember the night W. C. Parkey came over when my first piano was delivered to my house. He sat down and played the first tune. I will cherish that special moment forever. Robert Gilstrap would sit down countless times with me at the piano and show me musical fill-ins. He spent hours explaining music theory, a class I had been struggling with in high school. With Brother Gilstrap's help, I was able to pass with an A in music theory. I will be forever grateful that these mentors led me in the right direction and gave me the opportunity to do something for the kingdom of God. I believe music ministry was a great outlet for me through my teenage years.

I loved to sing and still do. My sister and I sang many duets together. We would practice and have a great time. My sister accompanied us on her guitar. I also sang some solo parts in the church youth choir, the infamous "Good News Singers." We even made a recording. Whether it was singing or playing, I was there and doing my part. This brought much happiness and relief to my heavy, sad heart.

These were the highlights of my teenage years. This is how everyone saw me. I was a friend to most, trying to see the good in everyone. But inside I harbored a deep fear.

Journal: *I'm so confused by questions that seem to have no answers. Why can't I control my emotions? God help me!*

Looking back on my teenage years makes me sad. Outwardly, I was always the life of the party, but inside I was empty and on a constant quest trying to find out who I was. I was always falling head over heels in love—or so I thought—with

> Borderlines soon learn to take and do whatever it is they need to soothe their scary feelings and silence their troubled minds.

boys much older than I, and consequently was obsessed with wanting to be older so my dreams could come true. I never paused to enjoy the moment. I was never satisfied with where I was in life. I had no idea the amount of harmful baggage I was carrying. That alone made it very difficult to enjoy life to the fullest.

I seemed to be a very likable person in my teenage years. If there was a party or a get-together of some kind, I yearned to be in the spotlight on center stage. I was not one to sit alone on the sidelines. I did, however, do that inside. In my spirit I was all alone.

I was allowed to go places and do things with guys and girls much older than I. My parents, who had no clue about the abuse, didn't realize how dangerous this was for me. One of the saddest things about sexual abuse is that you are extremely vulnerable to more abuse. I was aware there were boundaries and knew there was a right and a wrong, but where were they? My boundaries had been so grossly crisscrossed and misused that I couldn't find them. Neither could I distinguish between right and wrong. I am thankful God kept His hand on me.

I was always very tired. Mom didn't have to tell me to go to bed at night; I was already there and sound asleep. But night disturbances are common in a person suffering from sexual abuse. I had many horrific nightmares growing up, and they continued until I was a year into my healing. Many times I would wake up screaming, thinking someone was "getting" me. I was right—it was the fear monster.

My sweet mom suffered with numerous health issues and was in and out of the hospital the year I turned twelve. It continued like this for several years. They didn't quite know what the medical issue was with Mom, but she really suffered. Her brain was oxygen deprived due to poor circulation, and she would often faint or just fall. During one hospital stay she had a cardiac arrest. It seemed I never knew from one day to the next if I would have a mom or if God would choose to take her.

> I would wake up screaming, thinking someone was "getting" me. I was right—it was the fear monster.

Mom could not keep her balance and spent many hours on the couch resting. She wasn't able to do normal "mom duties," so my older sister stepped in. She was a great substitute, but I'm sure it was a pretty big task for a fifteen-year-old. She shopped for groceries, cooked meals, and cleaned house all while going to school and working a part-time job.

About this time my dad was starting a business and had to work very long hours. He worked his day job, then came home to work on jobs for his business. His day-job earnings had to support the family until his business began to make a profit.

I needed solid structure and daily schedules in order to cope, but my family didn't know this. We were just a typical family trying to get through tough times. I'm not sure how I made it through those years, but God knows. I'm so grateful He kept His hand on me and my family.

When you are sexually abused at such a young age, you don't develop emotionally, and you don't learn to communicate very well with words. Your emotional development stops at the age you were first sexually abused—for me it was age four. My communication skills were very stunted. In my mind, everything I said or thought was valueless. I mistakenly thought my body was the only important thing about me—what I looked like, how I carried myself, the way people viewed me. I never learned to value who I was as a person. I had no idea who or what I was meant to be.

On the outside I looked like I could not have been happier, but the laughter was a cover-up for the emptiness and loneliness I felt inside. Anybody would probably have been shocked to know what was happening to me and in me. Yes, I loved to laugh and party, but underneath the laughter was a miasma of pain.

Chapter 7

The Unending Cycles of Borderline Personality Disorder

Journal: *I think I'm doing okay, then suddenly it's winter. Please, God, I don't think I can make it through another winter. I'm dying a little at a time . . .*

I was driving aimlessly. Where? I didn't know. Just somewhere to get away from everybody and everything. Hearing people talk made me crazy. If only I could find a quiet place, maybe my mind would find peace. Where was all this headed? Would I totally lose it one day?

Tears were streaming down my face so fast I could barely see. Horrible thoughts raced frantically through my mind until it was tangled and confused. *Am I really a mother of six children? A wife? And—dear Lord!—a pastor's wife? How can I possibly be an example to a church full of ladies? If people knew the real me, they wouldn't love me, much less accept me as their pastor's wife, their leader, their guide, and their mentor.*

But no one could possibly know what a mess I was. I myself couldn't explain how I felt inside. It was like a terrifying, ugly force raging inside of me. I wanted to run away from everybody and everything. I hated to be and feel that way. Those off-the-wall notions slammed into me, seemingly out of nowhere. It was like being transported to another world, another time zone, another identity. There were no connections; nothing was attached; loose ends were hanging everywhere. Had I lost my mind? What was reality? Most of what I felt seemed so real, but it was far from reality. My world was a treadmill of pain and agony. I didn't think I could bear it any longer. The pain was such that I couldn't even explain. There was no cure, no one to talk to. If only I could find someone to make it all better for me, someone who had the answers to all my questions. But there was no one. Everybody was shut out. I didn't belong anywhere. I couldn't understand my own thoughts, so nobody else would be able to either. When I talked, the look on their face said, "You're not making any sense." This made me reluctant to talk to anyone. Why should I when no one understood what I was saying or thinking? The effort only made matters far worse.

I was driving fast, but where was I going? To a store? No. I wove in and out of traffic as if I have an important place to go and everyone was in my way. I ran through stoplights as though they didn't exist. Who cared if there was an accident? At least I'd be gone forever and wouldn't have to deal with this pain. My face was red and swollen from crying.

I felt an urgent need to go somewhere—to the water! Water had always sounded and looked so peaceful. Water rolled in and out, in and out, like my mind. No matter where my thoughts took me, I always seemed to end up where and how I started—angry. I would think, *I'm not really an angry person . . . but I'm so angry right now I could almost hurt someone!* But that only piled on more regrets and pain. Solutions to problems always escaped me. If only I could find a place where I could no longer hear the thoughts going through my head! My mind tormented me; the more anxiety I felt, the worse the torment. Maybe it would be better if I ended everything here and now.

Please, God, help me! All of my life I've heard about what You can do and what a wonderful thing it is to live for You. Can you hear me? Do you see me? Am I even a blip on your radar? Maybe not. Maybe I'm an infinitesimal piece of nothing floating through space, going nowhere.

Somehow I had to pull myself together, but I didn't know how so I just kept driving. I was a person with no purpose and no place to go. Yes, that was it. No place to go. I drove for miles and miles, stopping and pulling into parking lots or driveways to wipe my eyes because I couldn't see. Would I ever be able to figure out this thing called life?

I had made several futile attempts to figure it out: What had someone said that upset me? Why did I feel like a child? Why was I so angry? Why hadn't I ever really felt loved? Surely everything was not all my fault. Was something terribly wrong with me? Was there a real "me" or was I somebody else? The confusion was horrible, like being stuck in a busy intersection with cars honking, tires squealing, basses thumping, whistles blowing. My mind was spinning out of control.

My chest felt like it would explode. I pulled into a parking lot, making sure it was empty. I didn't want to be seen. I didn't want anyone asking if I needed help. I wanted to be left alone. I heard these childlike cries. I seemed to be standing to the side, watching myself pleading, *God, please help me! I think I'm losing my mind. Please, God, release peace into my mind.*

But nothing happened. God wasn't listening.

This was all too familiar; I'd been here many times before. I pounded the steering wheel, thinking it would help to relieve some of the pent-up emotion.

Sounds issued out of my deepest being, sounds I couldn't understand. I didn't know who I was or why I was born in the first

> "God, please help me! I think I'm losing my mind. Please, God, release peace into my mind." But nothing happened. God wasn't listening.

place. But wait! Something was happening. I was starting to feel a little bit calmer.

Then a sense of shame for my bad behavior rushed in. Things I said, feelings I felt. I started the car and began driving home to once again face the things I had done and the damage I had created. At home I pulled into the driveway ever so slowly, overwhelmed with a sense of shame. I felt like a child who has trouble explaining in rational terms why she feels a certain way. I really had no explanation. How had I become mired so deeply in the quicksand of life?

These wild cycles usually were triggered by something simple, something that didn't really matter. But they could last up to several days, and I would once again become detached from reality. I was so confused it was killing me. Why couldn't I understand what was going on? If only I could have found someone to help me, to tell me that I was suffering from classic symptoms of BPD. When I finally found that someone, the end of an episode always took lots of explaining and word pictures for me to finally understand what was happening. At this point, I would be so full of emotion I was like a dripping faucet. Even after all was made right and things were back to a semi-calm, I was still a long way from okay. I was so full of shame.

One of the most difficult aspects of Borderline Personality Disorder is the emptiness, the loneliness, and the intense feelings. The extreme behaviors kept me in a fog of confusion. At times I didn't know what I was feeling or who I was. When things finally settled down, I would lie awake, weeping for hours. I kept to myself because I wanted everyone else to think I was okay. The constant rewinding and replaying of these intense feelings and the accompanying adrenaline surges would leave me completely exhausted.

It usually took several weeks to several months to get back to what I felt was the "normal me." My self-esteem would plummet to the lowest depths with shame when I recalled the things I had done and said. Did any of it make sense? No. And it seemed I was back where I started.

Every person with BPD goes through similar cycles. They experience very few "good" days. A day might appear good on the surface, but down deep, emotions are churning and will at some point spew out. The best way I can describe it is to liken these cycles to the four seasons of the year:

Spring: Spring is a time of refreshing, regrouping, cleaning, and starting all over again. The birds are singing, the grass is turning green. There is a sense of new beginnings and putting the past behind. Everyone is tired of winter and looking forward to nice, calm weather after the winter storms. Spring is the most tolerable season, and the most welcome one.

The drawback for me was that moving from winter into spring was an ordeal. It was like carrying an unwieldy backpack and having to stop and rearrange everything in it in order to carry it comfortably and move on. Sharp-edged objects were poking me in the back every time I moved. Guilt and

> Every person with Borderline Personality Disorder goes through similar cycles. The best way I can describe it is to liken these cycles to the four seasons of the year.

shame were the worst; they reminded me of the past unkind comments and unwise decisions I had made.

But spring also was the time when I could make the best decisions and remember things I needed to do. This was when I was the most gentle, caring, considerate, and kind. It was when my mind was the least cluttered. I was less likely to become offended at constructive criticism or remarks. I could understand and converse at my best.

Springtime was always a time of regrouping for me. In the spring I would resolve not to veer in the same directions I had taken during the winter season. I felt I could get ahold of my mind and take control over my destiny, my path, and my everyday choices and decisions. If there was a season that I could choose to be in forever, it would be spring.

This was the only season in which I thought I could make it and would be able to move on, survive life, and conquer the world. If only springtime could last forever, maybe I could be successful at this thing called life.

Summer: But no matter how hard I wished for an eternal spring, summer always came. The freshness ebbed away, and the flotsam and jetsam of negative thinking washed in with the tide. Although I sometimes was able to stem the tide with something positive, slowly but surely my self-esteem would start to slip. I was distracted and unsure of myself. Disillusionment set in.

One of my most dangerous thoughts was thinking that I was just fine and everything that went wrong was *everyone else's fault*. Foisting the biggest monkey onto someone else's back made my little monkey easier to carry.

Through it all I was so blessed not to have developed an addiction. My way of coping was to escape somewhere, maybe to a store, a park, or some other peaceful place. These places were my refuge when the struggles began. The problem with the summer season was that I could see I was beginning to slip. Anytime my behavior was brought up, I became defensive. I would insist I was doing well, thinking it was true, but fall was coming . . .

Fall: By the time chilly fall started whisking the leaves off the trees, things were spiraling downhill for me. My mind churned up negative things people said and negative ways I had acted. My self-worth plummeted

Next to winter, fall was the season I hated most. I could see the explosion coming; I was becoming more nervous, more uncomfortable, and more inconsistent.

downward in a spiral. I still tried desperately to succeed in everyday life, but I found myself flailing about, trying to get away from the evil enemy pursuing me.

One of the worst symptoms of my BPD was the negative thoughts churning inside my mind seemingly at a hundred miles per hour. It was pure torment. I couldn't help myself. It was like seeing an oncoming car in my lane and there was no way I could avoid a head-on collision.

Next to winter, fall was the season I hated most. I could see the explosion coming; I was becoming more nervous, more uncomfortable, and more inconsistent. I lacked concentration. Fall was boxing me inside my own private world where I couldn't see anything but myself. Didn't people see the trouble I was in? *Please, somebody, I need help before the oncoming car hits . . .*

Then the raging winter would slam into me, cold and cruel.

BPD is unpredictable. You never know how long each season will last or what will trigger the cycle—flashbacks, emergency situations, or relational confrontations. Sometimes the restless, relentless winter seems determined to keep you from seeing spring. You must learn to weather it out no matter how unpredictable it may be. Life has to go on somehow, some way.

Chapter 8

And Then There's Deception

Now the serpent was more cunning than any beast of the field which the LORD God had made. And he said to the woman, "Has God indeed said, 'You shall not eat of every tree of the garden?'" And the woman said to the serpent, "We may eat the fruit of the trees of the garden; but of the fruit of the tree which is in the midst of the garden, God has said, 'You shall not eat it, nor shall you touch it, lest you die.'" Then the serpent said to the woman, "You will not surely die. For God knows that in the day you eat of it your eyes will be opened, and you will be like God, knowing good and evil." So when the woman saw that the tree was good for food, that it was pleasant to the eyes, and a tree desirable to make one wise, she took of its fruit and ate. She also gave to her husband with her, and he ate. Then the eyes of both of them were opened, and they knew that they were naked; and they sewed fig leaves together and made themselves coverings.(Genesis 3:1–7)

Journal: *I lay in bed that fretful night with tears streaming down my face. I was devastated beyond words, beyond comprehension, because of what I believed to be true . . .*

I would rather end my life than face the awful things I had done and said. The carnage was all around me. I knew I couldn't walk this road alone; it was way more than I could handle. *Oh God! Oh God!*

I am so grateful that God reached down into the garbage pits of hell to save me. If I had the courage to look back, I would see a cyclone behind me, ripping, hurling, killing everything in its path. It was like waking up in the

BPD wreaks havoc in a life, and can be deadly. Studies have shown that 70 percent of people diagnosed with BPD will attempt suicide at least once.

middle of a horrible nightmare only to find it was a brutal reality. I knew I could not fix my wrongdoing or restore anything on my own. I needed God desperately! Worst of all, I had caused hurt and pain to the people I loved most—my family, my church family, and my beloved husband and pastor. *Where do I even start, God?*

God sent His angels to minister to me that night. I know it's true because that's the only way I could have survived. I knew that gut-wrenching, soul-baring repentance was the only thing that would bring relief. The things I had done and said while entangled in the tentacles of BPD needed to be repented of. I'm so thankful God spared me and opened my eyes so I could see the hurtful things I had done, even the unintentional ones. I had to repent!

It is truly shocking to open your eyes and see the ugly things you've done staring back at you. You then realize what terrible things the human spirit is capable of doing. I had done things I would never have done had I not been mired in the swamp of BPD. BPD wreaks havoc in your life, and can be deadly. Studies have shown that 70 percent of people diagnosed with BPD attempt suicide at least once. I can understand why. Life was difficult enough with God; people without God have little chance of survival.

Deception is evil and insidious. It opens up a door that lets treacherous things in. It will take us to places we never wanted to go and make us say things to people that we never dreamed we would say. Deception is deadly. It comes from the "father of lies," an aggressor who will devour as many souls as he can through deception and then spew them out into a tortuous eternity. First Peter 5:8 (KJV) says, "Your adversary the devil, as a roaring lion, walketh about, seeking whom he may devour."

I cringe when I think how close I came to making some decisions that would have cost me family, friends, and, most important, my soul. I was on a deadly path, believing it was the only path I could take. I was deceived hook, line, and sinker.

Unfortunately, I made some decisions and accusations that created circumstances that will dog my steps for the rest of my life. But I still have God. I'm now on the right path, going the right direction. There are some things only God can fix. If we don't seek His help, our mistakes will drive us crazy and we will be continually trying to fix something that is unfixable.

Deception is nothing new; it debuted in the Garden of Eden. Deception led to consequences for which mankind has paid from that day forward.

> To the woman he said: "I will greatly multiply your sorrow and your conception; in pain you shall bring forth children; your desire shall be for your husband, and he shall rule over you."
> Then to Adam He said, "Because you have heeded the voice of your wife, and have eaten from the tree of which I commanded you, saying, 'You shall not eat of it': cursed is the ground for your sake; in toil you shall eat of it all the days of your life. Both thorns and thistles it shall bring forth for you, and you shall eat the herb of the field. In the sweat of your face you shall eat bread till you return to the ground, for out of it you were taken; for dust you are, and to dust you shall return. (Genesis 3:16–19)

Even though I made right everything I possibly could, some things were lost, never to be retrieved. So many people were involved that when wrongs were made right they could still choose what they would or wouldn't believe. Some were thankful for the healing God had done in my life; others chose to believe lies. I thank God for His grace and mercy

> Deception means believing something that isn't true; and worse, you don't realize you're believing a lie. It's a conundrum—an intricate, difficult, dangerous problem.

that brought me back to solid ground with a firm foundation. God is truly my Deliverer, Healer, and Refuge in the time of need. He heard my cry and knew just when to step in and do what He does best.

Deception means believing something that isn't true; and worse, you don't realize you're believing a lie. It's a conundrum—an intricate, difficult, dangerous problem. If we are truly honest with ourselves, we will have to concede that we, at one time or another, have allowed the devil to deceive us. Here are a few examples:

1. God does not love me.
2. I did not receive God's Spirit into my heart.
3. I'm never going to amount to anything.
4. If I can be good enough, maybe I'll make it to heaven.
5. I don't really have what it takes to live for God.
6. God doesn't want what's best for me.
7. I am not God's child.
8. God has not given me any gifts or talents.
9. I am a failure.
10. I am of no value to anyone.

It is one thing to think occasionally on lies like this. You might think about the lie for a short time, recognize it's not true, and struggle with it until you overcome it. It is another thing, however, to believe lies like this until your whole life becomes a lie. No one can tell you any different. This is a dangerous place to be. If you believe one lie, it's easy to believe another, and another, and another . . .

Staying in God's Word will help you not to believe a lie. II Corinthians 10:5–6 tells us, "Casting down arguments and every high thing that exalts itself against the knowledge of God, bringing every thought into captivity to the obedience of Christ, and being ready to punish all disobedience when your obedience is fulfilled."

If you don't cast down *every* deceptive thought as it comes through your mind, you will soon find yourself trapped in a stronghold of Satan. (See II Corinthians 10:3–4.) As a thought flits through your mind, you must determine, with the help of the Spirit, whether it is true or false. Is it your own human thinking, is it Satan speaking lies, or is it the almighty God speaking to you though your thoughts?

Learning to control your thoughts is one of life's most important lessons! Every battle starts in your mind before it ever comes out of your mouth. You live your life according to what you think. Your mind is a powerful thing.

> Learning to control your thoughts is one of life's most important lessons!

Those of us who grew up in apostolic homes may view deception as something a sinner deals with before coming to God. Or we may think a deceived person is someone who has strayed away from God and is no longer with us. This is true in many instances, but we need to look at ourselves. As soon as we think we can never be deceived, that's the most likely time for the enemy to attack. Failing to erect a hedge of protection around our thoughts leaves us vulnerable to deception. Or maybe we protect what we view as our weak areas to the neglect of our "strong" areas. Deception number one is thinking it will never happen to us.

Once we've let deception in, it puts down ugly, gnarled roots that spread rapidly throughout our mind. The devil gains a foothold before we even realize what is happening. How can we protect ourselves from the missiles the devil launches at us? The answer is to get up every morning and put our armor on—every piece. These are the tools God has given us to protect us from Satan's fiery darts.

I'm thankful I was never tempted to let down my beliefs and life of holiness. But many of us who question biblical truths seem to struggle through life, straddling the fence. The devil will entice us in all areas. If he cannot get us to fudge in one area, he simply goes to another. He knows every nook and cranny in which to gain a foothold.

Unfortunately, those who are suffering from BPD are fertile ground for deception. This personality disorder is full of volatile, immature emotions. The disorder is called "borderline" because the victim teeters on a tightrope, never fully falling off of either side. If something triggers an emotion, a Borderline can easily slip back to the age at which he or she was first abused. Here is an example of how it works.

> Sally complains: I can't seem to get anything done.
> Barb suggests: Well, maybe it would help if you wrote down a schedule or made a list.
> Sally explodes: You think my brain is so scrambled that I can't do anything right! You're treating me like a child! (Barb's suggestion has triggered Sally's emotions, and her mind rushes back to a four-year-old. Sally feels threatened; she feels she has failed. She has taken Barb's statement as a negative one and now feels Barb is against her. She bursts into tears.)

This conversation continues with Barb trying to figure out what she said that was so wrong. She insists she was only trying to help. Sally is devastated, thinking she has failed once again and is just a loser. Barb tries to explain over and over that she was only trying to help, while Sally hurls hurtful accusations at Barb: "You're always against me." "You don't think I do anything right!" "You've really hurt my feelings this time!"

Hours or maybe days later Sally's emotions flip to the other side. She realizes she took everything wrong; she was the one who said hurtful things, not Barb. She realizes she acted horribly to Barb and decides to apologize. Barb is left with a feeling of confusion, still having no idea what she did wrong, still thinking, *I was only trying to help. What happened? What was that all about*?

As the days go by, Sally flips back and forth, from thinking she was wrong for what she said and did to thinking Barb was definitely in the wrong. Barb was against her; she was the one at fault! Sally then becomes depressed, feels sorry for herself, and waits for an apology from Barb, which never comes. Barb has no clue she did anything wrong. She has no idea Sally has flipped to the other side. She will not know this until there's another blow-up and Sally brings up this conversation word for word, insisting how wrong Barb was.

This is a horrible way to live, for the one suffering from BPD, to the spouse, the children, the friends, and others within the Borderline's world. Unfortunately, the people closest to the person with BPD are the ones most affected by it. From the example of Sally and Barb, you can see how deception can enter into the picture. When all is said and done and the emotions have flipped back and forth, the Borderline usually concludes, "They were definitely in the wrong, and I was right to act and feel the way I did."

I can remember day after day of negative thoughts and emotions tearing through my mind like a tornado. I literally didn't know what to believe or which person to believe. I had to learn to fight negativity every day. Borderlines don't realize they are suffering from a personality disorder. It seems like a way of life, albeit a really hard way of life.

I spent most of the time wondering who I was and what I believed. This was because my beliefs changed constantly, flipping back and forth from the past as a child to the present as an adult. It was impossible to know which thought, feeling, or decision was right. My mind was a tangled mass of confusion. Deception moved in and felt right at home. It had won hands down. It was all too easy to convince my negative BPD mind that what I thought and felt was right on.

As you can see, the emotions I was dealing with were enormous. And the back-and-forth tug of war in my mind was a daily struggle. Then in the middle of each situation, there was the devil trying to sway me from one wrong side to the other.

That leads us to another dynamic concerning mental diagnoses and personality disorders. Having been a BPD sufferer, I've concluded that the devil considers people with these types of problems to be fertile ground for sowing seeds of deception. In my opinion, that may be why there is such a high rate of suicide due to conditions like depression, Bipolar Disorder, and BPD. It is easy for the devil to convince these precious people that death is the only way out. Their problems make it impossible for them to think straight.

Some feel that evil spirits are involved with mental diagnoses and personality disorders. Having gone through it myself, I strongly agree. I was tormented on many occasions and at times saw evil spirits in my house. Others cannot see the spirits, but they can sense the presence of evil. Nights were the worst.

> It was really hard for me to accept that my condition was attracting evil spirits. It sounded dirty and un-Christian.

Sometimes I awoke with a hair-raising scream, seeing evil faces or figures hovering over me. Or I would wake up to a dense cloud of spirits in my room. Deception invites evil spirits and entertains them. They feel welcome. It was hard for me to accept that my condition was attracting evil spirits. It sounded dirty and un-Christian. Thankfully, there is a difference in being "possessed with" a spirit and being "attractive" to spirits.

I believe evil spirits are attracted to a psychiatric floor in a mental institution or hospital. These poor, vulnerable people are suffering and struggling with illnesses of the mind, which become playing fields for the dark side. Satan plays dirty. He targets people who are hurting and defenseless; they cannot protect or help themselves. But there is a God. Yes, we have a God! And He always wins!

Please don't get tangled up in deception, because, should you manage to get out, the carnage left behind is often irreparable. Things are never the same again. For example, there are some family dynamics in my circle that will never be fixed. We all suffered some great losses because of deception.

Thankfully, God does restore in His time. He has a plan. Nothing has ever caught God off guard. He knew what was going to happen in my life, and He knows what is going to happen in your life. Things may look gloomy and you may not see a way out,but through experience I can tell you He will be enough for you.

Chapter 9

The Healing Process Begins

"The Sun of Righteousness shall arise with healing in His wings" (Malachi 4:2).

Journal: *I am determined to get through this. There is no turning back . . .*

"There is no turning back." I wrote those words on May 14, 2015. That's when my healing process began. It wasn't an easy journey. Like a baby taking its first steps, I had to learn the basic elements of a successful life.

1. Consistency
2. Patience
3. Perseverance
4. Persistence
5. Courage
6. Honesty
7. Pain
8. Tears
9. Life
10. Freedom

Romans 5:3–4 says, "And not only that, but we also glory in tribulations, knowing that tribulation produces perseverance; and perseverance, character; and character, hope." I think of this verse of Scripture when I look back on the last two-and-a-half years. It was a long, hard, but rewarding road to walk. You too can experience healing, but you will have to walk the road one step at a time. The journey will produce perseverance and character in your life. You will learn patience, for you must work at it consistently, day in and day out. This journey is not a cakewalk. It takes a person who has made up their mind.

Many times I asked, *Please, God, just come down and miraculously heal my mind. Oh please, create in me a new mind.* But this would have been the easy way out. I have seen or heard of very few times when God instantly and miraculously healed someone of all their past baggage and pain. He is well able to do that in a moment's time, but most of the time, He chooses not to.

> If God had reached down and totally healed my mind in a moment's time, it would have been difficult to cope with all the sudden changes. I would have missed the growth that has come into my life.

After walking the road of healing, I believe I understand why. Healing is like peeling an onion one layer at a time. If God had reached down and totally healed my mind in a moment's time, I would not have been able to recognize myself. I would have missed the growth that has come into my life. I would have missed all the "God moments." It would have been difficult to cope with all the sudden changes. It would have literally blown my mind! God knows what He's doing, and everything He does is perfect.

Physical healing, emotional healing, and mental healing contain several similar steps. Let's say you go to the doctor's office for a consultation for a hip replacement. You wince as he explains the process. You imagine the pain (or, as they say in doctorese, the discomfort), sweat, and tears you must go through in order to have that brand new hip and get it working as it's supposed to. After the surgery you wake up and find yourself hooked to an IV with a morphine drip; the pain level is such that they give you permission to push the button each time the pain exceeds what you can bear. After several days you move on to therapy. Ow, that hurts! But you must press on; you can't stop now. You must keep working at it for several months, or possibly a year, before you finally have the hip you were hoping for.

This is the way we must look at emotional healing. It hurts to talk to a counselor and work through all the pain, grief, and baggage that has plagued your life. It is very hard work to reprogram your thinking, but you have to! The day-in-and-day-out struggle with emotions and feelings makes you utterly weary. But the reward of healing, freedom, and deliverance is so worth the pain, tears, and hard work! You are no longer chained to the past. Your thoughts are clear, and you are able to make decisions with your head held high. You can do it!

My purpose in writing this book is to help those who are suffering and are desperate for answers. I want to take you with me on my healing journey. I am being transparent, for I want you to see that this journey is not a simple uphill climb until you reach the mountaintop of healing. There are valleys of great despair, times when you would rather give up and try to hobble your way back down, bruised and worn out. Times when you long to run away from reality and truth. I want you to know it is okay to get discouraged and depressed at times, and wonder when the journey is going to end. There's no shortcut; emotional healing takes time; it is a process. If you can stay the journey, there will be times you will grow by leaps and bounds, and other times you will struggle to take baby steps or even slide backward a step or two.

Every journey has its good times as well as the bad or difficult times. I wouldn't take anything for my healing journey—but neither would I want to walk it all over again. It was well worth it, and I'm grateful to my God and all He has done for me. I'm telling you this because I don't want you to walk into your personal healing journey, have some difficult struggles and then wonder, *Is it normal to have days like this?* It takes a great deal of courage and strength to push forward when you feel as though you are making no headway and have hit a roadblock or a speed bump. You must keep walking and pushing forward toward complete healing. It must not be *a* resort; it must be the *only* resort. You must realize it's more painful to stay as you are.

> If you can change your thinking, you can change your life!

I encourage you to start your journey today. You can do it. God is a God of life and freedom. Yes, you can do anything when you do it in the name of Jesus!

I believe the most important, life-changing truth I have learned is something you need to practice on a daily basis: *take every thought captive.* There is way too much "stinking thinking." Taking every thought captive is hard work, but if you can change your thinking, you can change your life.

1. It will free you up as nothing else can.
2. It will give you more energy.
3. It will correct your boundaries.
4. It will keep you in the Word of God.
5. It will make you aware of the thoughts you allow yourself to dwell on.
6. It will lighten your load.
7. It will reduce your stress level.
8. It will help you become Christlike.
9. It will teach you to depend on God.
10. It will set you on the right course.

You may have heard II Corinthians 10:5 preached and talked about all of your life, but has it really sunk into your spirit and wedged deep down into your heart like an anchor on the bottom of the sea? This was one of the first areas I had to tackle. A "stress-accelerated mind," or racing thoughts, is one of the many agonizing things a BPD sufferer experiences.

Imagine you are walking in the woods. You round a clump of bushes, and there in front of you stands a huge bear! Thoughts begin racing through your mind: *What do I do—run away? Which direction? Should I climb a tree? Or is my life going to end right here?* Adrenaline rushes through your body. Your senses are heightened. Your heart rate and breathing accelerate. Your pupils dilate. You are jittery and nervous.

For me, this happened nearly every day. There was no sense of order, no beginning, and no ending. It was very difficult to remember things, organize myself, and communicate properly while negative thoughts were racing wildly through my head. No wonder I felt like I was going crazy. I learned that the solution was to take every thought captive. It was the only way to work toward my healing. It was extremely hard at first, but as I persisted, it became easier.

You have to take *every* thought captive. That is the key to II Corinthians 10:5—taking every thought captive and lining it up to the Word of God. *Is this thought true? Is it positive? Is it uplifting? Is it going to help me in my walk with God?* We must weigh every thought on a spiritual balance scale, which is the Word of God. If it's not a good thought, we

> The key to II Corinthians 10:5 is to take *every* thought captive. We must weigh every thought on a spiritual balance scale, which is the Word of God.

must immediately erase it from our mind. It cannot be allowed to stay.

I had trouble deciding if a particular thought was my own stinking thinking or if it was from Satan. In either case, I said, "Satan, I rebuke you! I command you to leave my mind in the name of Jesus!" If it was Satan, the thought would leave immediately. If it didn't leave, I knew it was my own imagination. I would then begin to occupy my mind with good thoughts, God's Word, singing, or whatever it took. I had to learn techniques that helped me to change.

You will have to do the same. Whatever technique helps you may not be helpful to someone else. However, you know God's Word is always a great source. You must keep reading it until your mind is clear and at peace. I had to cry out to God many times. He would show up and do what He does best: my mind would stop racing and I would feel the awesome presence and peace of God.

Do you listen to your self-talk—your inner voice? Our thoughts are like a silent, internal chatter heard only by ourselves and God. Our self-talk affects not only our inner man and our spirit, but our physical health. It can be negative and self-defeating or cheerful and supportive.

> The mind of the wise instructs his mouth, and adds learning and persuasiveness to his lips. Pleasant words are as a honeycomb, sweet to the mind and healing to the body (Proverbs 16:23–24, Amplified Bible Classic Edition).

Have you ever heard someone say something and then end up with, "Oh my! Where did all of that come from?" It came from a thought. If it was a negative, unproductive thought, you know they had allowed themselves to dwell on it instead of taking it captive. What we think will eventually come out of our mouth in one form or another. Then it will translate into action.

We must remember that our choices and actions will not change until our mind does. That is a powerful statement, and it's true! That is why it is so important to take every thought captive.

Our thoughts affect our attitude. When we wake up in the morning, we can decide we are going to have a good day and make the best of it, or we can get up not caring about anything, come what may. Believe me, I know. It is hard work waking up when yesterday was a horrible day and you just don't have the strength to care anymore. You would rather throw in the towel. But you must get up, telling yourself, "I'm going to have a good day. God will help me through any failures or problems today. I can do all things through Christ who strengthens me!"

You have to learn to out-talk your mind. This probably sounds silly, but do you talk to yourself? I do. I've found

> Your choices and actions will not change until your mind does.

that when I say it out loud, I can hear plainly what I'm thinking. I know it sounds crazy, but try it. And tell yourself the truth. It works, and it is a great tool to use.

Another thought pattern to conquer is worry. We will worry every day unless we take every thought captive. It is impossible to worry and have peace at the same time. What does worry sound like? "God, I have a situation here. I'm going to worry about it until I get it figured out and come up with the solution I think is best. I really don't need Your answer or input. I think I can take care of it without You!" Worrying is a sin because we are becoming our own god and pridefully taking over God's job. We think we know better.

> Be anxious for nothing, but in everything by prayer and supplication, with thanksgiving, let your requests be made known to God; and the peace of God, which surpasses all understanding, will guard your hearts and minds through Christ Jesus. Finally, brethren, whatever things are true, whatever things are noble, whatever

things are just, whatever things are pure, whatever things
are lovely, whatever things are of good report, if there is
any virtue and if there is anything praiseworthy—
meditate on these things. The things which you learned
and received and heard and saw in me, these do, and the
God of peace will be with you. (Philippians 4:6–9)

Worry and anxiety are tactics Satan uses to attack our mind. God
did not create us to worry and stress about things. Our bodies cannot
handle worry, anxiety, and stress; they will do us harm. Billions of
people come down with a worry/stress-related illness every year.

An estimated 85 percent of illnesses are stress related. Many
times when people go to the doctor to get their aches and pains
checked out, the doctor cannot find a physical reason for it—because
their condition was brought on by stress. Many times heart attacks,
stomach issues, high blood pressure, depression, anxiety, and many
more conditions are caused by the worry and stress we have put on
ourselves.

We demolish arguments and every pretension that sets
itself up against the knowledge of God, and we take
captive every thought to make it obedient to Christ.
(II Corinthians 10:5, NIV)

When we fail to bring down imaginations, wrong theories, and
faulty reasoning, we are giving the devil a foothold; we are sending
him a signal, opening the door to him, and welcoming him in.
Conversely, when we strive to have the mind of Christ, we will bring
every thought into the captivity of Christ and cast down every
imagination as soon as it enters our mind.

Chapter 10

Accountability and Support System

Journal: *A new beginning—I need a new beginning!*

The two things essential to accountability are honesty and trust. This is, of course, very difficult for some people, especially those with BPD. In fact, for a Borderline, trust is one of the main struggles. Most counselors refuse to take on a patient diagnosed with BPD. They are frustrating to treat and a good percentage of the time they will refuse any more counseling after only a few months. This is the reason I can say my healing was truly a miracle!

The norm for me was a feeling people were out to get me. I couldn't handle criticism, no matter how constructive. As long as people agreed with me and understood me, I was okay. The minute someone started questioning what I thought or felt, I would back away, put a wall up, and many times lose it emotionally.

Support System

Spirit-filled Counselor: It is key to find a counselor you can be open and honest with. You cannot hold back any truths from them. If you can't be truthful with them, you will be wasting your time and their time. Yes, the truth will hurt. You will feel you've been stabbed in the gut. That's the very reason why you don't or can't come to grips with the truth—it hurts! You don't want a repeat performance. You don't want to try to process it. You don't want the counselor looking down on you because of what you did or said or thought. People are all too good at making excuses and pointing fingers.

But I want to tell you the pain of telling the truth is worth it. The truth will make you free! This pertains to all truth. Anytime you find out the truth about anything, it is freeing. You no longer have to wonder what the truth is; you no longer have to wander in the unknown. When you know the truth, it can then be dealt with and processed in the right way. God wants all of us to know all truth. We should strive to know the truth about everything. God is truth!

Your problems are not news to God; He already knows everything about you. He also knows that

> "You shall know the truth, and the truth shall make you free" (John 8:32).

you need the help of a professional counselor to walk you through the healing process. When you arrive at the realization that you need help, and you have found a counselor, why not be open and honest? It will benefit you greatly. Once you make openness and honesty a habit, it will help you to remain that way. Truth is a very crucial element to your healing and recovery.

I thank God that He put an apostolic, God-led professional counselor in my life. Here's how it happened.

I had scheduled Vani Marshall to come and speak at our February 2014 Sectional Ladies Conference. She came, and we had a fantastic time. Many received the Holy Ghost and ladies were refreshed and blessed. Vani Marshall later told me that during our communication and throughout the conference sessions she felt things were not all right with me. As I was chauffeuring her back to the airport after our conference, I began to open up to her about issues in my life. I admitted I needed help. But as most people with BPD do, I didn't see myself as the problem. I pointed my finger at others. I would find out in due time how wrong I was . . .

If you are suffering from BPD, it is essential that you find a professional counselor who is apostolic. I repeat: this is a must! Yes, I am partial to Vani and would recommend anyone to go to her for counseling. She saved my life, with the help of the Lord! You must look for a Spirit-filled counselor who is experienced in helping people with your type of problem. Dealing with it can be very tricky. BPD doesn't fit into the category "if you've seen one, you've seen 'em all." Every case is different because every person is unique. Vani Marshall is educated and has studied BPD. Furthermore, she has extensive experience in many fields, but this one as well. Please don't go to a counselor who is not educated in the field of your need. This too is vitally important.

If you are concerned with finances, I can tell you that receiving my healing was worth every penny my husband and I spent. Granted, nobody really has the money set aside for counseling, but I encourage you to look at BPD as you would a physical condition or illness. If you need surgery, you somehow come up with the money to pay for it. In addition, my experience with people has taught me that when you pay for something, you will most likely follow through with the professional's instructions. Freebies are usually a waste of time and energy on both sides. The bottom line is you cannot afford not to get the counseling and help you need. Anything that improves your human relationships and your walk with God comes with a cost. You cannot put a dollar amount on your soul.

What I'm about to say will be controversial to some people. First, let me say I believe God can do anything! He has reached down and touched my mind many times. But unfortunately, I've heard people and/or ministers tell those suffering with emotional issues that all they need to do is pray more. "If you will just pray, you can get through this. You can conquer this problem."

As humans, we have a body, soul, and spirit. We will go to a doctor for our medical needs and think nothing of it. Why don't we do the same for our mental/emotional needs? I believe God can direct a professional counselor to what we need in mind and spirit as well as He can direct a doctor performing surgery on our body. It is unfortunate that a certain stigma seems to plague those suffering with emotional/mental problems and issues. Don't let the label distract you. The only thing that matters is what God thinks.

The labeling comes with being uneducated about mental and emotional issues. Some will turn you off; they don't want to know or hear anything on the subject. Sometimes they avoid the issue because they have hurts buried deep within themselves and the subject is too close for comfort. Others will claim there is no such thing as depression. Some are against medicating a person with a mental illness. I understand and realize some people may be overmedicated, but if they had the chance to work through their past and unload their baggage, they would get to the place where they no

> We will go to a doctor for our medical needs and think nothing of it. Why don't we do the same for our mental/emotional needs? I believe God can direct a professional, apostolic counselor to what we need in mind and spirit as well as He can direct a medical doctor performing surgery on our body.

longer need medication. I believe we should make every effort to do what we can for ourselves, along with the help of God, so we don't have to rely on medication. However, I also understand that some have no choice. We take medication for high blood pressure and other illnesses and think nothing of it. Possibly we wouldn't have to take as much medication if we altered our lifestyle and changed our diet.

I want to encourage you to step out and go get the help you need. God will place a hedge of protection around you. You are not alone. God will restore you.

Vani and I had many God moments during our counseling sessions. I remember one time when she was working with me on forgiving the person who had sexually abused me. As she painstakingly took the time to instruct me on how to do this and in what order, the glory of God filled the room. It was as if God had poured a bucket of compassion inside of me. I leaned over and began weeping tears of compassion. Vani looked at me in amazement and said, "Jodie you have already forgiven. The process is already done!" This was only one of the many miracles God performed in my life.

> The glory of God filled the room. It was as if God had poured a bucket of compassion inside of me. I leaned over and began weeping.

Numerous times I would tell Vani things that I was working through, and she would say, "Jodie, do you realize that is a miracle? People with BPD don't think like that. They can't process like you just did! It's a miracle!" Thank you, Jesus, for all those times. Now I know You truly care about me.

Counseling required that Vani and I adjust our schedules so I could get the hours and treatments I needed in order to heal. I was in Kansas City and Vani was in Louisiana, so sometimes I flew there, and sometimes my husband and I drove. It took a lot of scheduling in order to get the face-to-face counseling sessions I needed. Vani also conducts sessions over the phone or online, but I found that being with her in her office worked the best for me. In between sessions, if I needed to talk with her on the phone or by text or email, she always gave me a golden nugget I could use to get over a hurdle.

Pastor: My pastor, Stan Gleason, showed me bucketfuls of grace, mercy, care, and concern. Even when I was struggling and wasn't the easiest person to pastor, he was a true shepherd looking out for my soul and had my best interest at heart.

Being under the protection of your pastor is a must. I was very fortunate to have a pastor who was understanding and supportive. Getting spiritual counsel from your pastor will help guide you and lead you in the right direction. It is a great advantage to both of you when your pastor is part of your support system and knows what you're going through and how you're progressing. Your pastor may not fully understand your condition, but don't let that discourage you. He or she is a vital part of your support system. Your pastor was called by God to be your leader and guide, and he is accountable for your soul. He loves you!

Accountability Partner: The last vital element of your support system is an accountability partner. It is essential to find a friend that holds you accountable. My beloved husband was the friend who walked with me through twists and turns, ups and downs. If I came to a fork in the road, or it was pouring down rain, or I was wading through a waist-high creek, where was he? *Right by my side*! He trudged up every mountain and walked through every empty field with me. He held my hand when I cried buckets of tears. He has been my strength and my support. He has literally walked to hell and back with me.

Before that, I never knew how strong love could be. He taught me how to love when all he could do was stand still and hold me until love flowed out of every part of him. I have no words to explain to what great lengths my husband sacrificed for me and for my very soul. He truly lived out Ephesians 5:25: "Husbands, love your wives, just as Christ also loved the church and gave himself for her."

Then the crisis came. My BPD peaked. I was done, and it was over. I walked out of the house and left everything. I lost all comprehension of what I was doing and what I was thinking. I was totally deceived. The day I walked out, my husband lost everything and suffered things I don't even have the words to describe. He literally gave his life and his ministry to save me and help me all that he possibly could.

Gone was our house; we had to sell it. Gone was the church my husband had pastored for twenty years. Gone was the men's ministry he had led for about twelve years. Gone was our income. We even lost some of our relationships. It was like my husband was another Job; he lost just about everything there was to lose. I could not have made it without him by my side, encouraging, strengthening, and guiding me along the way. Vani Marshall helped and counseled my husband through the process. She gave him the knowledge he needed to help guide me through.

I realize this may not be possible for you. The friend or family member you choose as an accountability partner must acquire a great deal of knowledge about BPD so they won't lose heart in their efforts to help you. If they don't have the knowledge, it will be very detrimental to you and hinder the progress of your healing. Therefore, it would be in their best interest, as well as yours, to be involved in some of your counseling sessions.

> Your accountability partner must be someone who is with you most of the time and can watch how you communicate. He or she must be aware of your emotions and attitudes and reasoning. You must be able to trust this individual with your feelings, thoughts, fears, and failures.

Your accountability partner must be someone who is with you most of the time and can watch how you communicate. He or she must be aware of your emotions and attitudes and reasoning. You must be able to trust this individual with your feelings, thoughts, fears, and failures.

When I say trust, I mean blind trust. At times I struggled with truth and facts versus emotion. My emotions were so intense that my whole body was telling me they were right. That's why it's important for you to be able to trust your friend when he or she tells you you're not thinking right, lays out the facts, and shows you where your thoughts are going astray. Your friend can see when you are dissociating, can watch your "cycling," and help you by letting you know what he or she is seeing. Trusting this friend is very hard. At times you will fail, but your friend will be there for you through the worst of times.

Your friend will hold you accountable—no more dishonesty, blaming others, or pointing fingers. You must learn to take responsibility for every action and every word. This alone will let you see how dishonest you really are with yourself and others. This will shed a whole a new light as you dig deep beneath the surface and into your heart, soul, and spirit.

> Search me, O God, and know my heart; try me, and know my anxieties. (Psalm 139:23)

Another great benefit of having an accountability partner is being able to talk out your feelings and thoughts. There were times I would sit and talk to my husband, and before the conversation was over, I had answered my own questions. My frustration would be gone and I would feel at peace with myself. Talking things out with a trusted friend is of great value. It is harmful to leave thoughts and feelings tangled up in your mind. The pileup will soon become too much to deal with.

That's why I say you must pick your accountability partner very wisely. A wrong choice can lead you down the wrong road. This person must be very strong and healthy emotionally and mentally. An unhealthy person cannot work with you correctly.

When you see your need for healing, I urge you to choose your support team wisely and then begin. It's a long but vital journey. It will be worth every tear, every heartache, and every penny spent. You will become free and view life from a different perspective. You will become whole in Jesus Christ!

Chapter 11

Identity: Who Am I?

For You formed my inward parts; You covered me in my
mother's womb. I will praise You, for I am fearfully and
wonderfully made; marvelous are Your works, and that
my soul knows very well. My frame was not hidden from
You, when I was made in secret, and skillfully wrought
in the lowest parts of the earth. Your eyes saw my
substance, being yet unformed. And in Your book they
all were written, the days fashioned for me, when as yet
there were none of them. (Psalm 139:13–16)

God saw us the very moment we were conceived. No one had
any idea we were there except for Almighty God. He knew us before
we were born.

It follows, then, that *we* need to find out who we are—not just in
our minds, but deep down in our hearts. Many people have the head
knowledge of who they are in Christ, but the reality hasn't sunk into
their heart and spirit. They have not accepted that God actually
formed them in their mother's womb and chose them.

For instance, take our bodies. We must accept every part of our
bodies because God made them. We must look at all of our
imperfections and realize this is the way God wanted us to look and
to be. He doesn't make mistakes. So how do you think it makes Him
feel when He sees us fretting over the size and shape of our nose? Or
how tall or short we are? Or the color of our hair? It must make Him
sad when we question His handiwork. We need to become content
with how God made us because we were fearfully and wonderfully
made.

We often struggle with jealousy because someone else was given
a talent that we don't have. We want their talent and wish we could
give ours away. We are forever comparing ourselves to someone
else. This brings us unnecessary grief because we are not thankful
and content with the talents and gifts God has put within us.

He created and designed the type of personality we would have.
He even knew our idiosyncrasies. I believe He blessed us with

talents and gifts according to our personalities and makeup. He knew how much we would be able to handle. Some can handle only a small amount of responsibility, while others are Energizer Bunnies. Some can handle being in the spotlight while others prefer to work behind the scenes. Some work well on their own while others enjoy working with a team. Whatever and whoever we are, God designed us as a personalized, perfect package.

If we are trying to do things that are not our natural bent, talent, or gift, and they don't turn out, we wonder why we don't succeed. Could it be are striving for something God did not intend for us to be or become? We must learn to use the talents and gifts God has given us. I'm not sure God will bless what He didn't put in us. When we attempt to do or be something we're not, we are working against what God meant for us to be. It's no wonder that we come to a dead end, discouraged and wondering why things ended up that way. God will always bless and work through anything that He created.

Can you imagine living life not knowing who you are or anything about yourself? Can you imagine not knowing what your name is or who your parents are? What would happen if you walked into City Hall to pay your taxes? The clerk would ask, "What's your name?"

"I don't know," you would answer.

"Then what's your address?"

"I don't know."

(If you're a lady), "What's your maiden name?"

"I don't know!"

It is sad that many people don't know who they really are, and thus find it impossible to live an overcoming life. For instance, if a person is sexually abused, as I was, they become disconnected emotionally from their body. They lose a sense of who they are. They are like strangers to their own body. They must learn who they are before they can have a proper relationship with God.

Below is a list of Bible verses that I started reading every day— and still do—in order to instill them into my spirit. These Bible verses identify who I am in Christ.

Who Am I in Christ?

I am accepted:

John 1:12	I am God's child.
John 15:15	I am Christ's friend.
Romans 5:1	I have been justified.
I Corinthians 6:17	I am united with the Lord, and I am one spirit with Him.
I Corinthians 6:19–20	I have been bought with a price. I belong to God.
Ephesians 1:1	I am a saint of God.
Ephesians 1:5	I have been adopted as God's child.
Ephesians 2:18	I have direct access to God through the Holy Spirit.
Colossians 1:14	I have been redeemed and forgiven of all my sins.
Colossians 2:10	I am complete in Christ.

I am secure:

Romans 8:1–2	I am free forever from condemnation.
Romans 8:28	I am assured that all things work together for good.
Romans 8:31	I am free from any condemning charges against me.
Romans 8:35	I cannot be separated from the love of God.
II Corinthians 1:21–22	I have been established, anointed, and sealed by God.
Colossians 3:3	I am hidden with Christ in God.
Philippians 1:6	I am confident that the good work God has begun in me will be perfected.
Philippians 3:20	I am a citizen of heaven.
II Timothy 1:7	I have not been given a spirit of fear but of power, love, and a sound mind.
Hebrews 4:16	I can find grace and mercy in the time of need.
I John 5:18	I am born of God, and the evil one cannot touch me.

I am significant:

Matthew 5:13–14	I am the salt and light of earth.
John 15:1, 5	I am a branch of the true vine, a channel of His life.
John 15:16	I have been chosen by God and appointed to bear fruit.
Acts 1:8	I am a personal witness of Christ's.
I Corinthians 3:16	I am God's temple.
II Corinthians 5:18–20	I am a minister of reconciliation for God.
II Corinthians 6:1	I am His coworker. (See also I Corinthians 3:9.)
Ephesians 2:6	I am seated with Christ in the heavenly realm.
Ephesians 2:10	I am God's workmanship.
Ephesians 3:12	I may approach God with freedom and confidence.
Philippians 4:13	I can do all things through Christ who strengthens me.

These verses have been invaluable tools in my life. After I pray in the morning, I turn to these verses and read through the entire list. It's vitally important to my spiritual well-being that I get these truths into my spirit and heart before I check any social media or email. The Word of God is the bread of life; I need the spiritual nourishment it provides in the early morning hours. I take time and meditate upon each verse. When I hear the still, small voice while I am reading the Bible, there is no doubt it is my heavenly Father. There is nothing like hearing that calming, peaceful reminder that God is with me, sees me, and acknowledges me as His child.

I suggest that you read these verses and take them to heart every day. They will help you discover your identity. They will bring freedom to your spirit. They will change your life.

It builds self-esteem to know who you are, who your Father is, that you were bought with a price, and that your Father is preparing a mansion for you on the streets of gold.

You cannot earn God's love. He loves you for who you are. When a baby is born, Mom and Dad are so excited as they hold this screaming, wet scrap of humanity! Love—unconditional love—sweeps over them. Their newborn has done nothing but cry; it has done nothing to earn their love, but they love their baby!

God loves you! You don't have to keep track of how many times you attend church, how long you pray, how many days a year you fast, or how kind you are. You can simply say, "I am God's workmanship. I am His temple."

The following verses of Scripture became milestones on my journey to wholeness:

1. "No longer do I call you servants, for a servant does not know what His master is doing; but I have called you friends, for all things that I heard from My Father I have made known to you" (John 15:15). This is worth thinking about until it sinks in. Yes, He is my heavenly Father, but He is also my friend. I like to compare this to my earthly friends. My friends love to spend time with me; they laugh with me, they don't mind helping me out when I have a need, they pray for me when I'm sick, and they love me even when I mess up. God is that kind of friend to me. He is a friend that sticks closer than a brother. That is pretty awesome!

2. "Having predestined us to adoption as sons by Jesus Christ to Himself, according to the good pleasure of His will" (Ephesians 1:5). This tells me that He chose me. I didn't become God's child just by happenstance; He chose me. He wanted me. He looked at me and said, "Yes, I will take her. I will lead and guide her as My own." What a privilege! I am blessed!

3. "For through Him we both have access by one Spirit to the Father" (Ephesians 2:18).

I can call out to God anytime I want or need to, knowing He will answer me. I have God's telephone number!

Many times we compare our heavenly Father to our earthly father, and for some, this doesn't make sense. If they had a gruff, hardnosed, abusive father, they may see God in that light. If their father was distant, they may feel as though God is a million miles away and has no time to hear their prayers and concerns. Some don't even know who their father is. But if you can let these verses soak into your spirit, they will make a difference in your life.

4. "And you are complete in Him, who is the head of all principality and power" (Colossians 2:10). This verse has helped me to see that if I have God every day, I am complete. I am not a misfit. I'm not lacking. I am a complete package deal. I am the temple where He resides. God can do anything and everything, and I can't do anything without Him. He has chosen to work through me; I am God's tool.

> I am not a misfit. I am not lacking. I am a complete package deal. I am the temple where God resides. God can do everything, and I can't do anything without Him. I am God's tool.

5. "There is therefore now no condemnation to those who are in Christ Jesus, who do not walk according to the flesh, but according to the Spirit. For the law of the Spirit of life in Christ Jesus has made me free from the law of sin and death" (Romans 8:1–2). Some days we wonder why we feel so condemned and why we are struggling so badly in our mind. It's because we have reached over and taken out from under the blood the things we have repented of. We are walking in our flesh. The Bible says there will be no condemnation if we're walking according to the Spirit, which means God is in control and we have the mind of Christ. Then we will have no condemnation. Unfortunately, it is all too easy to slip back to the carnal way of thinking and start agonizing over everything we did or said. We must realize when this happens that we are bringing it all on ourselves. We are letting condemnation rain over us and saturate our spirit. But we must get back up, pull ourselves together, and remind ourselves that our sins are all under the blood. If we will do our part, God will always do His part.

6. "And we know that all things work together for good to those who love God, to those who are the called according to His purpose" (Romans 8:28). I used to think this meant God was only going to allow good things to happen in my life. But it says *all* things work together for good. God's purpose is for us to make it to heaven. This means He is not concerned when our life down here is not a bed of roses. He will take anything that happens, whether we deem it good or bad, and work it out for our good so we can make it to heaven.

The tough, hard times He allows are supposed to help us grow and become mature in Christ. Instead, some become bitter. I want to tell you to keep your chin up! God loves you and wants to see you at the marriage supper of the Lamb. Allow everything God sends your way to purify your spirit. It will be worth it all!

7. "Being confident of this very thing, that He who has begun a good work in you will complete it until the day of Jesus Christ" (Philippians 1:6). This verse encourages me in that He will faithfully finish in me what He has started. I'm sure there have been times when God has had to put things on hold because I wavered off the path. He patiently waited until I decided to get back on. I'm sure there have been times He has allowed things to happen so I would realize where I was and what I needed to do in order to have the mind of Christ. God has a plan for each one of us. So keep walking, growing, and learning.

8. "For God has not given us a spirit of fear, but of power and of love and of a sound mind" (II Timothy 1:7). God does place upon anyone a spirit of fear. This tells us that anytime we are fearful of a situation or a person, we know it is not from God. In working through BPD, there were times I did not have a sound mind. Satan loves to sneak up on us and catch us unaware. In those times I would read this verse out loud, sometimes over and over. We must do this to reclaim a sound mind. To obtain healing I had to totally reconstruct and reprogram my thinking process through the Word, prayer, counseling, and different types of therapies. Through it all, God has proven to be faithful to His Word.

9. "Let us therefore come boldly to the throne of grace, that we may obtain mercy and find grace to help in time of need" (Hebrews 4:16). I can't count how many times I've quoted this verse. I had to learn to be totally dependent on God. With BPD, I felt vulnerable, weak, and useless. When I first started the healing process, it was really hard for me to lean on God, to go to Him every time I had an emotion or an issue I couldn't handle. This caused me to feel even weaker and more out of control; I wasn't able to help myself.

> With BPD I felt vulnerable, weak, and useless. I had to learn to be totally dependent on God. Now I can't wait to run to God for grace and mercy and help in the time of need.

But as I worked through the healing, I soon learned God loves it when we come running to Him. He said, "My strength is made perfect in weakness." Our heavenly Father loves to show up and become our strength. Then in our weakness, He gets all the glory. Now I can't wait to run to God for grace and mercy and help in the time of need. I know I cannot live a day without Him.

10. "I am the true vine, and my Father is the vine-dresser. . . . I am the vine, you are the branches. He who abides in Me, and I in him, bears much fruit; for without Me you can do nothing" (John 15:1, 5). When I started reading this passage, verses 2–4 caught my eye. Verse 2 says, "Every branch in Me that does not bear fruit He takes away; and every branch that bears fruit He prunes, that it may bear more fruit."

In spite of my struggles with BPD, God had used me in several areas in the gifts and talents, such as the gift of prophecy, tongues and interpretation, and music ministry. I was always careful not to add or take anything away, but as the BPD spiked, I later learned there were several "words from the Lord" I had given to a few people that missed the mark. This devastated me; I had never meant to mislead anyone. I was so ashamed and embarrassed that I drew into a shell and wouldn't come out. I realized I needed to heal.

One day John 15:2 started speaking to me. I realized that if I refused to let God use me, He would pluck my branch off of the vine.

But later, when my husband and I started evangelizing, people kept coming up to me and thanking me for various words I had given them. Their kindness would encourage me. I found that out of the six to seven years God had used me in this area, there were just a few "words from the Lord" at the end that had missed the mark. Besides that, there were hundreds of words that God had given me that were a great help to people. I realized I had allowed the devil to tell me that because a few "words from the Lord" were faulty, all of the words I had spoken were wrong. Satan's lie had devastated me, and I didn't ever want to be used in that area again.

But one day John 15:2 started speaking to me. I realized that if I refused to let God use me, He would pluck my branch off of the vine. I can't say I'm totally there yet, but I'm stepping out to encourage and help others. I don't want God to pluck out a gift He intended for me to use for His glory.

I shared this story to encourage you not to put away the gifts and talents the Lord has given to you. Yes, there will be times you need to heal and rest. But be strong and of good courage; you will come back. God will use you wherever and whenever you allow Him to. God restores, and for that I'm so thankful!

11. "For we are His workmanship, created in Christ Jesus for good works, which God prepared beforehand that we should walk in them" (Ephesians 2:10). It means everything just to know we are His workmanship. We are important to God. He continues to work on us and in us on a daily basis.

12. "In whom we have boldness and access with confidence through faith in Him" (Ephesians 3:12). I can approach God with confidence and freedom, knowing He will help me. The only strings attached are bonds of love.

13. "I can do all things through Christ who strengthens me" (Philippians 4:13). If there is a verse I have used more than any other, it would be this one. On the days I didn't think I was going to make it, I would repeat this verse, sometimes in my mind, sometimes under my breath, and sometimes out loud. I said it over and over.

These verses became my source of strength, and with that came hope. If you really want to heal, get better, and grow, read them on a daily basis because consistency matters. These verses are like tools in a tool chest. Pull them out and use them.

Chapter 12

Repentance: Humbling Oneself before God

Journal: *Oh my Lord, forgive me! I have said some harmful words, and others are suffering because of it. They are playing the things I said over and over in their minds like an old phonograph needle on a broken record, and the scratches won't heal. I'm so sorry!*

The process of change begins with honesty, which is a form of repentance. Repentance is an internal shift from denial and rebellion toward truth and surrender.

We all repent as we pray each day. We repent of the sins we can think of off the top of our head and the sins we committed that we weren't even aware of. That's great. It is necessary to do that. But in this chapter, I'm defining repentance as a dying out to our flesh, possibly something we've never done before.

> Repentance is an internal shift from denial and rebellion toward truth and surrender. It is a dying out to our flesh.

I will never forget my groanings and tears of repentance. Sometimes I didn't think I would last through the night. God opened my eyes to see into places in my heart—secret places that were too evil, grimy, and ugly to contemplate. It would do no good to plead for mercy on the grounds that I had done all of these things under the influence of BPD. They were still wrong, and oh so deadly!

I could never undo the bad decisions I had made; they were gone forever. I didn't think I could live with myself, even though at the time I said those ugly things I believed them to be true. I couldn't contain it all; it was too overwhelming. Would my fountain of tears ever dry up? Would this nightmare ever be over? Maybe everybody would be better off if I never woke up.

You can see that a person suffering from any kind of emotional disorder or addiction does not think straight or act correctly, although they don't realize it. But there is still a right and a wrong, and there always will be. People have to pay the consequences, even for unintentional crimes. They still have to repent.

When we come to God in repentance, there are no more excuses and finger-pointing. We must approach Him all alone, with our faces to the ground. I have found that only when we become humble and broken before God will He begin to do a work in us that only He can do.

In repentance we become an open book. God already knows the contents of our book; but He wants *us* to read it. Repentance is a hungry, broken return to God. It flows out from the shock of learning the wrongs we have committed against ourselves and others and God.

The expression goes, "Say nice words because you may have to eat them!" I found that to be true. Eating all of those words was horrific. They had a vile taste, and the aftertaste was even worse because I knew I could never retrieve them. Words are either life or death; they will lift up or they will tear down.

As I lay there agonizing during the night, I realized how deceived I had been. I prayed, *Oh God, please forgive me for my rebellion. I never knew my heart could be so evil!*

Repentance often begins with dissatisfaction. We are miserable; we are ready for change. We don't care anymore what the consequences or the outcome will be. We are ready to humble ourselves before God and start our journey into completeness.

We suddenly realize we are living our life to *give* and not to *get*. We put away our agenda of what we think life is supposed to be. We give up our rights for the sake of the cause of Christ. God said, "Take up your cross and follow me." We must be able to lay everything aside and say, "Not my will, but Thine be done."

Repentance is a death that leads us toward a resurrection. Abused people have died inside; their emotions are wrapped tight and buried deep. Repentance requires the digging up and unwrapping of those emotions. That is a very difficult task for a wounded person, but once it is done, it frees them from the grave clothes, and they can open up their hearts to

> Abused people have died inside. Their emotions are wrapped tight and buried deep. Repentance requires the digging up and unwrapping of those emotions. Once that is done, it frees them from the grave clothes, and they can open up their hearts to love and relationship.

love and relationship. God strengthens our purpose. He grants us tenderness toward other people. True repentance will always lead toward coming alive in order to help others for their well-being and to the glory of God.

Genuine conviction and repentance take us from self-centeredness to other-centeredness, soften our heart, and help us to see we are no better at our core than the one who abused us. Jesus Christ died on the cross for our sins. He forgave us. The least we can do is go to the place in repentance where we see ourselves as no better than the abuser. The Cross is a leveling ground where we see that we all are capable of doing the unthinkable. In *The Wounded Heart*, Dr. Dan Allender maintains that repentance, for the sexually abused victim, involves both internal and external shifts:

The Internal Shift of Repentance

The internal shift of repentance involves three areas:

1. I refuse to be dead. A victim lives with a dead soul and spirit, which to her makes perfectly good sense; being dead kills off all the hurt and pain. Being dead blocks out all memories of hurtful words said and deeds done to her. This, however, deadens her to relationships. She is nothing but an emotionless robot. She slogs through life as if it's a requirement rather than an honor to be alive and enjoy life.

When an abused person refuses to be dead, she acknowledges and embraces her existence. Being alive gives her permission to feel her past as well as her future. She becomes open toward God and begins to develop a close relationship with her Creator. Opening her heart will initially bring sadness, grief, disappointment in herself and others, and sorrow. The difference is, she will no longer blame herself; she will be able to move on.

Sadness will open her heart to what life was meant to be but is not. *Grief* will bring the past alive, and she can admit the abuse was real. Grief mourns for what was lost that can never be regained, and exposes the hardness and anger in her heart from assigning blame to others. Godly *sorrow* and repentance bring her heart to a place where it becomes tender and pliable. God can begin to do some surgery on her heart.

93

When she gets to this place, she has a choice: she can say, "Never again will I allow myself to be abused, victimized, and misused for someone's selfish gratification," or she can say, "I was abused and mistreated, but I also see the wrong things I have done and how I treated others because of the abuse. I choose to repent of my wrongdoings and continue on the road to life, freedom, and a healthy relationship with God and others."

2. I refuse to mistrust. The opposite of mistrust is caring. After a victim has been abused and mistreated, she cannot be expected to trust the abuser or ones who have harmed her. But the breaking of repentance softens her heart, and she begins to care about the person or persons she could not trust. She learns how to pray for her abuser.

This stage of the process must be approached with caution, however. The victim must be careful she isn't putting God in the category of someone to mistrust. Some will direct their anger toward God for the abuse and blame Him for allowing it to happen. The reality is that sin and abuse exist in this world. God created mankind with a will of his own, so God cannot be blamed for the bad and harmful choices some people make. However, when we trust and love God, He can take the things in our lives that were meant to destroy and make them turn out for our good.

3. I refuse to deny physical passion. A refusal to deny passion embraces both pain and pleasure. Embracing passion enables a victim to feel the emotion, pain, and pleasure of deep relationship. These things are wonderful, desirable, and God-given. But a fear of physical passion keeps the victim from developing any deep relationships. Many times abuse victims will feel closer and safer around their pets than around people. A pet poses no threat of intimacy and closeness. They can pick up their pet, hold it, and cuddle it with no strings attached. They view emotional and physical passion as very dangerous areas because they bring back nightmarish thoughts. Passion makes them feel dirty. It's an area they don't ever want to revisit. It's like returning to the place where unpleasant, degrading things happened. It's a cruel reminder. It takes a great deal to get past this to reach the place where a victim can experience passion and intimacy as God intended close relationship to be. It is difficult, but it can be achieved.

The External Shift of Repentance

The core of all change is internal, but the evidence of it will shine externally like a morning sun bursting with energy. Repentance is an active choice to turn back to God. Repentance is all about truth in the inward parts. Repentance puts the bad choices and messed-up situations in a different light—the light of truth. Things become transparent. It's as though God opens a door or sheds light on something you couldn't see before. Repentance changes your thinking and decision-making. Your past, present, and future are now juxtaposed; you can look back at how you used to think or how things used to be and at the same time look forward to a transformation. God is great at transforming situations in a way you never dreamed possible. The goal is to move away from self-protective patterns, which seems really simple but it takes a lot of work.

"But as many as received Him, to them He gave the right to become children of God, to those who believe in His name" (John 1:12). Repentance brings a fresh awakening and a new start. All of our relationships will begin anew.

Repentance has one central quality: a hungry and humble heart that moves toward God. God will respond to heart-hunger and will lift us up. We begin to recognize that life emerges from brokenness and humbleness toward God.

Repentance opens our heart to hunger for our Father's love and embrace. It brings a fresh awakening and a new start. All of our relationships will begin anew. I promise you. Weeping may endure for a while, but joy will come in the morning!

Chapter 13

My Lifeline: Prayer and My Bible

Journal: *Prayer and the Word have really sustained me today . . .*

> Blessed be the LORD, because He has heard the voice of my supplications! - The LORD is my strength and my shield; my heart trusted in Him, and I am helped. (Psalm 28:6–7)

Prayer is a powerful part of our life; it is a lifestyle. Mother Teresa said, "Prayer is not asking; it is putting oneself in the hands of God, at His disposition, and listening to His voice in the depth of our hearts."

Everything else in our life is or should be centered on prayer. We must feel as though we can't live without prayer because if it weren't for God, we wouldn't be. He is the reason for our very existence. Our prayers should

> Prayer is not asking; it is putting oneself in the hands of God, at His disposition, and listening to His voice in the depth of our hearts. –Mother Teresa

include elements of confession, adoration, submission, petition, repentance, and praise to God.

Prayer is confessing our sins. We must humbly repent of our sins every day, even the ones we are unaware of. We must be broken and come before Him with openness and honesty. We made some bad choices; now we must come clean. There's no smoothing anything over or excusing our bad attitudes and behaviors. God doesn't expect us to grovel at His feet begging for forgiveness, but if we want forgiveness, it is imperative that we forgive others. "And forgive us our debts, as we forgive our debtors" (Matthew 6:12). After we open our hearts and confess, it sets us in the right direction and frame of mind.

Prayer is relationship. The first word that comes to mind when I think of prayer is "relationship." Relationships can be close or casual, but our relationship with God must be the most important one.

My closest human relationship is with my husband and soulmate. Each day we give ourselves to each other selflessly. We don't think twice when one of us needs something. But our relationship with God should trump that relationship. We should feel as though we cannot go a minute without thinking about Him or breathing a few words to Him.

Do you ever wonder what God is up to? If He's thinking about you? What blessing or miracle He is sending your way? What it will be like when you see Him face to face? Your relationship with God should be an exciting one! You don't need to wonder if He is looking out for you. In fact, He keeps many illnesses, accidents, and unfortunate circumstances from your door unbeknownst to you. That is just how much God thinks and cares about you. You ought to care as much about Him. Do you get up, pray your scheduled prayer time, and then forget about God the rest of the day? Acts 6:4 (KJV) says, "But we will give ourselves continually to prayer and to the ministry of the word."

Prayer fills that deep desire to be with God. When we talk with God, we align our spirit with His. When we walk in His Spirit, we are Christlike. We will make decisions throughout the day with the mind of Christ. "Rejoice always, pray without ceasing, in everything give thanks; for this is the will of God in Christ Jesus for you" (I Thessalonians 5:16–18). Praying always means we draw near to God in everything we do. It means praying about everything we do and involving Him in every decision we make.

When we keep God at the forefront of our mind, we are much more likely to be walking in the Spirit. If we encounter a situation that requires a decision, it's much easier to make a Christlike decision if we're walking in the Spirit. Communing with God aligns our thinking with His. We will have peace and comfort knowing we are choosing the best option. We won't be second guessing ourselves.

We become like the people we spend the most time with. Have you ever noticed that you will pick up little sayings or a pronunciation of a word from someone you're around a lot? Your thoughts become their thoughts. For instance, you know what they're going to say before they say it, and vice versa. You've probably heard someone say the longer a couple is married, the more they begin to look alike. The old saying goes, "Birds of a feather flock together." When we spend every day with God, His character rubs off on us.

Prayer is asking in order to receive. Thank God, all we have to do is ask! How hard is that?

> Ask, and it will be given to you; seek, and you will find; knock, and it will be opened to you. For everyone who asks receives, and He who seeks finds, and to him who knocks it will be opened. (Matthew 7:7–8)

The problem is that many times we neglect to ask. What do we do when we need a quick answer about finances, a medical need, or some conflict resolution? We get on the telephone and call someone for help or advice. Sometimes we just feel a need to vent with no purpose other than someone listening to our issues and problems. We don't really want an answer, we just want someone else to worry and fret with us.

One of our biggest mistakes is getting so busy and distracted that we don't take the time to ask God. We then become our own god and make a carnal decision. Any decision made without consulting God is a mistake and will leave us without peace.

God wants us to be specific and sincere when we come to Him in prayer. However, we need to be careful what we ask for, because we may find the answer is something we really did not want or need.

> You ask and do not receive, because you ask amiss, that you may spend it on your pleasures. (James 4:3)

He already knows what we need, but He wants to hear it from us. When we are close to God and we ask for things with the mind of Christ, our list will be a lot different than if we ask carnally. And though we all tend to want an instant miracle, instant relief, and instant answers, we can't always expect that.

Sometimes I would ask God to give me a revelation or an understanding of a situation. It wouldn't come immediately but as I walked through the day, keeping my heart and mind focused upon God, boom! A thought would come to mind and I would realize it was the answer. What a refreshing surge would rush through my spirit! Peace and understanding would saturate my soul. Nothing is more exciting than to be refreshed and encouraged by God.

Other times I was desperate and pleaded with Him to protect my mind, to give me strength to make it through another day. Now that I've been on this road of healing and recovery for quite some time, I realize God won't do everything for me. He only expects me to do what I know to do. It's called working together with God in relationship. A true relationship is not one sided; it must be give and take. I learned to work together with God by doing everything I knew to do, taking every thought captive, keeping my mind on Christ, taking care of my body with what I eat, and getting the rest I need. I can't walk half-heartedly through the day expecting God to do everything. He doesn't work that way.

One of the hardest lessons for me to learn was consistency. I was not and still am not consistent by nature; every day I have to concentrate on walking with God, praying before I do anything else in the morning, and being mindful of Him throughout the day.

God knows each of His children and what each one needs in relationship with Him. What I mean is, if you have children, you don't treat them all the same. You don't talk to them the same way. Each one of them responds to you differently. That is how God is with us. He knows how we need to be helped and corrected.

Prayer is sharing our thoughts with Him. Just as we share our thoughts with family and friends, God loves for us to share our deepest thoughts and feelings with Him. Yes, He already knows our thoughts, but He loves to spend time with us and hear our voice.

Emptying out the things and situations that worry us and giving them to God opens the door to faith. If we truly give our troubles and cares to God, we expect God to take control of them and do with them what He sees fit.

We all have problems that are out of our control no matter how we've tried to avoid them. But God has asked us to cast our cares upon Him. He knows our bodies can't handle the weight of all our cares—including the cares of our family, friends, coworkers, community, and the world! Giving God everything allows us to empty our minds, then, as the thoughts creep back in throughout the day, we can take every thought captive.

Prayer is praising Him for who He is. Do you ever forget your own needs and just lavish words of endearment and praise on God? He loves to hear your voice telling Him what an awesome God He is! Find out what I mean by reading the psalms of David. He knew how to bless God with praise and adoration. He knew how to praise God for who He is! "God, there is none like You! You are magnificent! You are powerful! You have always been and always will be!"

Prayer is thanking God for what He has done for us. There is nothing like having a thankful heart. Daniel knew how to lavish thanks on God for what He had done.

> I thank You and praise You, O God of my fathers; You have given me wisdom and might, and have now made known to me what we asked of You, for You have made known to us the king's demand. (Daniel 2:23)

My heart is full of thanks for what God has done in my life, especially during the last three years. Some people use the word "thankful," but their thanks does not issue out of their heart or spirit. They say "thank you" because that's what one is supposed to do. The minute we realize and believe we can't live that minute—or any other minute—without God, it makes us truly thankful.

The song "I've Been through Enough to Know He'll Be Enough for You" means a great deal more to me now than it ever did before. I know God saved me from the pit of hell, and He can do the same for you. If I didn't believe that, I wouldn't be writing this book. I wouldn't be revealing my testimony—my life story—to you if I wasn't thankful for what God has done for me and if I didn't believe my God can do the same for you!

He continues every day to touch my mind and heal and touch yet another area of my thinking. He heals me of things I don't even realize until He gently brings them to my attention. What an incredible God!

I get so thrilled and excited writing about the miracle God has done in my life! I know God did not single me out; I'm no more special than anyone else, but He treats all of us as if we're special. We are His jewels. I'm so grateful Jesus thought I was worth saving!

Prayer is declaring our dependence on Him. This one took me awhile because of the BPD. It was hard to admit I was dependent on God. A person with BPD has the feeling that her thoughts and feelings don't really matter. Sexual abuse has left her feeling vulnerable and helpless because she had no choice. She hates feeling so scattered and insecure and childish. Nothing God could do would make her feel any better, so why crawl to Him for help?

But through healing and prayer and the Word of God, I now love being God's child. I love to depend on Him. I can't wait to ask Him, "God, what do you think about this?" I love knowing I can't live one day without Him, and, even more amazing, is that He doesn't want to live one day without me! Part of my prayer every morning is, "God, I can't live one day without You. I have to have You today!" That makes me feel secure. Throughout the day, as the need arises, all I have to do is reach over and grab His hand. How awesome is that?

I encourage you to become dependent on God. He will never let you down or give you a wrong answer to any situation. He is a prayer-answering God!

Meditation. Meditation is a vital part of prayer.

> Let the words of my mouth and the meditation of my
> heart be acceptable in Your sight, O LORD, my strength
> and my Redeemer. (Psalm 19:14)

What if, in our relationships with people, we did all the talking and never listened to what the other person had to say? That person would think we didn't care about his or her opinions and feelings. They might conclude that we think we know everything. The friendship certainly wouldn't be fair or fun.

How do you think God feels when you get through saying everything you want to say and then leave Him standing there with His mouth open getting ready to speak something into your life with nobody there to listen? You have shut His words out of your life.

Meditating upon the Lord has become one of my favorite things to do. I love to think on things that are true, noble, just, pure, lovely, and of good report. Many times I find myself going to a quiet room, lying on the floor before God, and opening my mind and heart to what He wants to tell me. I don't think about what I want to say to

Him; I just lie quietly, submitted, humbled, and waiting on God to lay something on my heart. It's peaceful just lying there thinking about great victories and all the miracles God has done in my life.

Isn't it nice when someone says, "I'd rather be with you than anyone else right now, so I'm going to sit here and enjoy listening to your heart and what you have to say." Don't you think God loves it when we take time out to think on things pertaining to Him and open ourselves to what He wants to put in our heart?

God has often given me direction and answers while lying quietly before Him. It teaches me how to wait patiently (Isaiah 40:31). Isn't it nice to just sit in a quiet room with God? To bask in His presence and feel His arms holding you tight? One day I was sitting in my husband's church office when it literally felt as if God was giving me a bear hug. The sensation was so vivid I can still feel it. God will give us whatever we need. He will always do His part as we do our part.

Prayer is spiritual warfare. Prayer is fighting against the rulers of darkness.

> For we wrestle not against flesh and blood, but against principalities, against powers, against the rulers of the darkness of this world, against spiritual wickedness in high places. (Ephesians 6:12, KJV)

Being in the throes of emotion, confusion, or conflict gives the devil a perfect opportunity to weasel his way in. Once inside, he stirs up emotions that deceive, confusion that makes it impossible to think straight, and conflict that causes turmoil and distraction. We end up places we didn't intend to go.

Evil spirits can cause mental torment. I finally learned how to recognize them as the enemy and come against them. I believe people sometimes would rather blame the devil than take responsibility for their own wrongdoing. Whether or not it's the devil, we must assume responsibility and do what it takes to correct the problem.

Satan plays dirty. He takes advantage of people suffering from depression, addictions, emotional imbalances, mental problems, and personality disorders. He certainly took advantage of me.

Your mind is your most complex organ. If you're already struggling with wrong thinking, Satan considers it an invitation to move in and attack, and he invites other spirits to join him. Negative thinking is the opposite of faith, peace, and joy. It is not uplifting; it will drag you down. Don't get me wrong; I don't think people who struggle in this area are inferior to people with strong, sound minds. I'm simply saying that Satan plays dirty.

Anytime there is confusion in your mind, or you walk into a place of confusion and conflict, please understand the devil is at work. (See I Corinthians 14:33 and James 3:16.) Our God is not the author of confusion; He is the Prince of Peace!

Because of my experience with BPD and learning how Satan works, I have become aware of many spirits. When I was a young adult struggling with depression and BPD, there were times I was aware of an evil presence in the room, although at the time I didn't know what was going on. Now that I know and am older and wiser, I sometimes go through my house anointing doorways and praying in each room of my house, commanding any bad spirits to leave in the name of Jesus. The late missionary Nona Freeman spoke about this subject when she ministered at our church. She said, "Everything you do, do it in the name of Jesus!" "Whatsoever ye do in word or deed, do all in the name of the Lord Jesus, giving thanks to God and the Father by him" (Colossians 3:17, KJV).

I often had to deal with a spirit of heaviness. Sometimes praying and reading my Bible would not make the spirit go away. I would then bind the spirit of heaviness and release the garment of praise (Isaiah 61:3). Instantly, praise would sweep into my spirit, and I could command Satan to leave in the name of Jesus. My mind would become peaceful and the confusion would leave. I would begin to think clearly.

Don't be afraid of binding and loosing. Even if you aren't dealing with a spiritual attack, nothing is lost. No harm has been done. You simply must try other resources in order to bring about resolution and peace in your heart and mind.

Another element I have had to bind at times is a spirit of fear. When a spirit of fear would come over me, I would shake as if I was very cold. I was frozen in my tracks. I couldn't think straight. I would lose faith and trust. Fear comes from trying to handle everything on our own and not allowing God to take care of it. But God didn't make us to operate that way. We have so many God-given resources; we must learn to use and apply them daily.

> When a spirit of fear would come over me, I would shake as if I was very cold. I was frozen in my tracks. I couldn't think straight. I would lose faith and trust.

So every morning I "plead the blood over my mind." What an important resource!

Bible reading. I love to read my Bible. It is one of the most peaceful and powerful things to do. How can we grow in wisdom and knowledge? How do we draw closer to God? How do we discern God's heartbeat? Every answer that we have ever needed is in the Word of God.

One of my favorite Bibles to read is *The Soul Care Bible: Experiencing and Sharing Hope God's Way* (American Association of Christian Counselors, Tim Clinton, executive editor). This Bible has much insight to offer. It has helped me in every area of my life. Most of the chapters have a heading that tells what the chapter is about. Whatever I was struggling with, whether it was depression, hope, grace, forgiveness, or attitude, the study was already laid out and I could find it easily and fast. For instance, see Jeremiah 29:11:

> For I know the thoughts that I think toward you, says the LORD, thoughts of peace and not of evil, to give you a future and a hope.

Not only did I often receive comfort from this verse, but there was a small study laid out to encourage me in the Lord.

There are many other good translations and study Bibles, but I would encourage you to stick to the King James Version when studying doctrine and holiness. If you like a good story, read *The Message*; it reads like a dramatic story and can be almost humorous at times.

Let's say you're dealing with forgiveness and turn to the awesome story of Joseph. Line up his story next to your story. Do they match? Are you forgiving the way God intended? Are you following each step? I have found that if I'm walking close to God, I will be aligned to His Word.

When you're reading the Bible, and maybe rereading a particular passage several times, be sure to keep an open mind. All of a sudden God will shed new light on the passage and give you understanding you've never had before. When this happens, highlight the passage and jot down a note so you can refer back to it when you need it. Soon you'll have accumulated many passages that can speak to you in a crucial moment.

One of my favorites is Psalm 46:10: "Be still, and know that I am God." This verse has spoken to me many times. When I encountered a situation I didn't understand and couldn't fix, I would read this verse. Sometimes we can't fix what's wrong; we don't have an answer. But when we're still and waiting on God, out of nowhere He will step in and bring peace to our spirit. We must have patience. God's timing is perfect. I would say most of the time we feel the situation will never be resolved; that is, until the crisis passes and we look back to realize how God stepped in at the perfect moment!

Reading the Word of God helps us to refocus and reengage. It brings all our thoughts and feelings to one place. It helps us to regroup our minds and bring every thought into captivity.

Chapter 14

Forgiveness

Journal: *God help me to forgive as Joseph forgave.*

The power to forgive comes to us as a divine gift. We choose to forgive, but God empowers our forgiveness.

I was in my car, on my way to forgive the one who had caused me so much pain—the one who had sexually abused me as a young girl. The secret that had been hidden for so many years was about to be exposed! I prayed, *God, please help me to do this right.*

I was both excited and nervous: excited because I was, once and for all, forgiving the one who had caused so much grief in my life, and I was hoping he would accept me and be set free and forgiven. Then the whole thing would be under the blood and put behind us both forever. I was nervous because this subject had never been brought out into the open prior to that day. What if this person denied doing it or was angry because I was bringing the subject up to his face? What would I do then? How would I react? All I could do was place it into God's hands, obey His Word, and leave the rest to Him.

I knew the devil would fight against my efforts of reconciliation. He hates forgiveness because it takes away all his leverage. Unforgiveness is one of his favorite tools to bring us down. The bigger the event, the more ferocious the fight. But thank God we aren't responsible for what the adversary does; neither are we responsible for the reaction or response of the person being forgiven. We are responsible for doing what God is prompting us to do.

It is important to remember this, because not every story will turn out like this one did. There were other times that I sincerely apologized only to have the other party react with unkind words. The consolation is, if you have done all you can do with a clean heart, then put it in God's hands and leave it there. Don't pick it back up.

As I drove, my mind drifted back to a few days earlier in Vani Marshall's office. She had been prepared to lead me through the process of forgiveness, knowing it would be difficult on this level. But God had other plans! It was almost as if He stood over me and poured a bucket of compassion into my heart like a flood. I began sobbing so uncontrollably I couldn't even say the words "I forgive." Vani watched as God did the work in me and exclaimed with wonder, "Jodie, you have already forgiven him!"

I was nervous because this subject had never been brought out into the open prior to that day. What if this person denied doing it or was angry because I was bringing up the subject to his face? What would I do then? How would I react?

I had never felt so much compassion for someone in my entire life! It was as if God had washed my heart inside and out and even waxed it until it sparkled in the sunlight. It was an indescribable moment, and I didn't want it to end.

With this memory etched in my mind, I continued driving to our meeting, basking in the feelings I had felt those few days ago. I knew God was going before me to help.

As I pulled up to the meeting place, I thought, *Am I still going to walk in and forgive him for what happened forty years ago? You bet I am!* I had thought out very carefully what I wanted to say. I wanted to be kindhearted, gracious, and merciful. I wanted to be Christlike.

I walked in and greeted him. We did some small talk, during which I tried to set the stage with kindness, friendliness, care, and concern on my part. I was careful not to do or say anything that would ignite fear or anxiety. Finally I brought up the sin from the past with only enough detail for him to remember and know what I was talking about, being careful not to give the impression I was bringing it up to cause embarrassment and shame. I told him he didn't even have to say anything, but I was forgiving him of everything. It was under the blood and I wanted him to be free of the sin and any thoughts and horrible feelings that remained. Tears flooded our eyes.

I cannot describe the good feeling that filled my heart. I'm sure he was feeling relief and freedom as well. We were surrounded with freedom and warmth. This was a divine appointment that I'm glad I didn't miss. I will never be the same again!

This was a divine appointment that I'm glad I didn't miss. I will never be the same again!

I learned that forgiveness done God's way is not an emotion; it is a willing act or decision. Here are some important elements to consider:

Repentance: We've already discussed repentance in a previous chapter, but I would like to reiterate an important point that must not be overlooked. We must come before God in repentance before we start down the road of total forgiveness. Repentance aligns us with God. We look at ourselves as no better than the person we need to forgive. We must go to the foot of the cross with a broken spirit before God. We will see then that we have sinned and hurt other people with our words and actions. We have also come up short.

If we try to forgive someone before we've come to God in repentance, even if our motive is to bring peace and forgiveness, we will not approach that person with the right spirit and attitude. We will be thinking only of everything they have done to us. We will think it's all about keeping score of everything they did to hurt us. We are upset with them. The monkey is on their back! They need to do so-and-so and such-and-such before we will feel they are really, really

Repentance and forgiveness go hand in hand like soap and water. This is hard for some to understand because we want justice for ourselves and an apology from them without looking inward into our own spirit. We want the reward without any work on our part.

sorry. We want to tighten the screws until they break under pressure. We let them see our anger and how upset we are. After all the damage they have done to us, they better be groveling at our feet, begging for mercy! Deep down in our hard hearts we want them to pay. We want them to feel the same pain they inflicted upon us.

Repentance and forgiveness go hand in hand like soap and water. This will be hard for some to understand because we want justice for ourselves and an apology from them without looking inward into our own spirit. We want the reward without any work on our part.

I don't know about you, but if I have offended someone in a bad way, I sure hope they come to me with a soft and broken heart and show me some mercy and grace. Even if they won't excuse what I did, I hope they will understand and are able to put themselves in my place.

God gave us a mandate to forgive.

> Be kind and compassionate to one another, forgiving
> each other, just as in Christ God forgave you. (Ephesians
> 4:32, NIV)

> Bear with each other and forgive one another if any of
> you has a grievance against someone. Forgive as the
> Lord forgave you. (Colossians 3:13, NIV)

What is true forgiveness? Author R. T. Kendall, in his book *Total Forgiveness*, offers the following list of ten aspects of true forgiveness.

1. True forgiveness is being aware of the wrong but choosing to forgive. We can't start forgiving if we truly don't recognize and accept what the person has done to us. Yet we don't want to dwell on the extent to which this person went to hurt us because we don't want to re-experience the pain. When we can acknowledge what they did to us and choose to forgive them anyway, we are ready to start the forgiving process. We have just made a Christlike decision. We are kissing revenge goodbye. We have crossed over into a supernatural realm where we choose to forgive.

2. True forgiveness is choosing not to keep track. The New International Version says that love "keeps no record of wrongs." You may be more familiar with the verse in the King James Version:

> [Charity] doth not behave itself unseemly, seeketh not
> her own, is not easily provoked, thinketh no evil."
> (I Corinthians 13:5, KJV)

Do you know someone who keeps track of wrongs? I do. This someone is still following the tracks of things done to them fifty years ago. Most of the time people keep records so they can throw it up in someone's face at a moment's notice. It helps them feel better about themselves: "I haven't done anything nearly as bad as what they did!"

Instead of keeping track, we should acknowledge what someone has done, but then get rid of it before it takes up permanent lodging in our heart. Letting it go will prevent bitterness from metastasizing in our inner man. The only protection we have is to take every thought into captivity every time the memory of the offense comes to mind. Let it go on purpose.

3. True forgiveness is refusing to punish. It is imperative that we let go of the thought of the wrongdoer not getting what they deserve and the fear that they will not have to pay for what they did to us. That kind of fear is the opposite of perfect love.

> There is no fear in love; but perfect love casteth out fear: because fear hath torment. He that feareth is not made perfect in love. (I John 4:18)

Fearing that God won't give our enemies what they deserve is like trying to take God's place. If we step in and take God's place, He steps out of it and that's all we get. God is grieved when we do this. We forget that we cannot possibly see everything God is doing. Just because we can't see it doesn't mean He isn't working on it. God knows how to "spank" His children in ways we would never dream. Give this process to God.

4. True forgiveness is refraining from broadcasting the wrong. I think it's therapeutic to talk to a counselor or a trustworthy person who will hold what you tell them in confidence without holding any offense against the person that offended you. In this context, revealing to a counselor a trespass against you in order to get some help is okay. It helps the counselor get to the core of the hurt.

However, if you are truly forgiving, you will not tell anyone else about the wrongdoer's offense. Doing so would be gossip. Gossiping is an attempt to lower the value, credibility, and character of your offender, and it reveals your desire for revenge. By the time the story gets passed around to a few people, it's sounding pretty bad. You must check your motive and make sure you are sharing for the right reason.

5. True forgiveness is showing mercy. "Blessed are the merciful, for they shall obtain mercy" (Matthew 5:7). Just looking at this verse makes me want to show mercy, because, God knows, I really need mercy! Our carnal nature wants others to suffer the consequences of what they did, yet when we do something wrong, we want God to show us mercy.

Showing mercy is being Christlike. "Be merciful, just as your Father is merciful" (Luke 6:36, NIV). When God should be meting out justice to us, He instead grants us mercy. He expects us to do the same for others. With that comes a blessing: "The merciful man doeth good to his own soul" (Proverbs 11:17). Let's show mercy!

6. True forgiveness is accompanied by grace. You show grace by what you don't say, even if what you could say would be true. True forgiveness is not taking a bold stand against your enemy even when you are in the right. Another word for graciousness is gentleness. Some want people to see what the offender has done to them and know, in no uncertain terms, that they themselves were in the right! Graciousness withholds facts about your enemy to keep from scarring their reputation. Remember pulling someone else down means stooping to their level.

7. True forgiveness is an inner condition. Forgiveness must take place in the heart or it is worthless. "Out of the abundance of the heart the mouth speaks" (Matthew 12:34). If we harbor unforgiveness in our heart, it will eventually come out. Conversely, if we have really forgiven, our gracious words and actions will show it.

Have you ever heard someone say, "I've forgiven this person; I don't hold anything against them, *but . . .*" then they proceed to give a detailed description of the wrong they have done. The very fact that it's pouring out of their mouth is a sign they have not forgiven. If we have forgiven in our heart, it doesn't matter to us what our enemy does or how he reacts. We are at peace; we will have victory; and we won't demand a certain action. Even if the enemy is showing no signs of being sorry, we are confident in our relationship with God and that we have been Christlike.

111

8. True forgiveness is the absence of bitterness. You can smell bitterness miles away! Bitterness shows itself in many ways, such as a short temper, high blood pressure, irritability, sleeplessness, a constant negative perspective, and a general feeling of unease, melancholy, or depression. Have you been around someone who has nothing good to say about anything? You can be sure they are choosing to stay bitter. Anyone will become bitter if they don't prevent thoughts of revenge and hurt from replaying in their mind. You know bitterness is gone when there is no desire to get even and you truly want the offender to do well in all that he does. Refusing to become bitter opens the door for God to give you peace and joy.

9. True forgiveness involves forgiving God. We do not realize it at first, and some of us will never admit it, but our bitterness is traceable to a resentment of God. This can be unconscious anger, meaning we are not aware of it. The rationale for this is that God is all powerful and controls the universe; therefore, because He allowed pain and misfortune to enter our lives, it is His fault. No one knows the full answer for this, but I think if we knew the reason why we were suffering, there would be no need for faith. But we do know this:

> All things work together for good to them that love God,
> to them who are the called according to his purpose.
> (Romans 8:28, KJV)

God turns evil into good for those who love Him—but only if we allow it. If we are willing to wait and allow God to work everything out for our good, we will see that He is good! When we're tempted to think He is being unfair, we must remember all things are equal with God—He is always fair. His intention is to get us to heaven. The things He allows will help mold us and groom us for that wonderful day.

10. True forgiveness involves accepting God's forgiveness. This means you must let yourself off the hook. You must see and accept that God has truly forgiven you. Too many people are walking around thinking they don't deserve God's forgiveness and consequently carry a heavy load of guilt and shame. They are convinced Jesus died on the cross for other people's sins, but not

112

theirs. Their sins were so monstrous that God's blood couldn't cover them! The sad truth is that if they cannot accept God's forgiveness, neither can they forgive someone else.

Besides the ten aspects of total forgiveness, R. T. Kendall also gives an insightful account of how Joseph was able to forgive his brothers for their treacherous treatment of him as a teenager. As a side note, it is interesting to discover the importance God placed on Joseph's story of abuse and ultimate forgiveness by comparing the allotment of space in the Genesis narrative: The first thirty-six chapters of Genesis cover significant events—Creation, the Flood, the Tower of Babel, the calling of Abraham, the destruction of Sodom and Gomorrah, and the life of Jacob—spanning *2,102 years* of Bible history. At chapter 37, however, the narrative slows dramatically with the account of Joseph's brothers selling him into slavery. Except for chapter 38 (the story of Judah and Tamar), the remaining twelve chapters of Genesis deal with the life of Joseph from his teenage years until his death, a span of only *92 years*. That's an approximate ratio of 20:1. It is almost as if God introduced Joseph's story with the phrase "I said all of that to say this . . ."

The Story of Joseph

One of my favorite stories on forgiveness is the story of Joseph. I get teary-eyed every time I read it. Joseph's life is the perfect example and guide to go by. I used Joseph's gentle yet powerful story as a guide for my journey toward forgiving my offender.

Joseph had good reason to wallow in self-pity. What would you feel like if your brothers ridiculed you for your dreams of future leadership? Or hated you so much they sold you into slavery? What if you were taken to a foreign country, never to see your homeland again? What if your brothers told your father you were dead, causing him untold grief? What if you were falsely accused and thrown into prison? What if the person who promised to get you out forgot all about you? All of these things and more happened to Joseph. He had plenty of reasons to harbor bitterness in his heart.

But I believe God was at work softening Joseph's heart to bring him to a place of forgiveness. During the seventeen years or so Joseph waited and worked in Egypt, he held on to the dream that someday his brothers would bow down before him. I believe that God sometimes has to wait a long time for our heart and attitude to change so He can accomplish His will in our life. I would like you to apply Joseph's example by studying the following list of dos and don'ts.

1. Don't tell anyone what someone did to you or said about you. At the climax of the story, Joseph waited until everyone had left the room before he revealed his true identity to his brothers.

> Then Joseph could not restrain himself before all those who stood by him, and he cried out, "Make everyone go out from me!" So no one stood with him while Joseph made himself known to his brothers. (Genesis 45:1)

An overwhelming compassion must have swept over Joseph at this moment. We can be sure he had this all planned out because he didn't want any member of the court to know what his brothers had done to him. He knew if anybody found out, his brothers would be punished. He wanted his entire family to be with him. He assured them, "No one will know. I will take care of you." This is how God is with us. "As far as the east is from the west, so far has He removed our transgressions from us. . . . I, even I, am He who blots out your transgressions for My own sake; and I will not remember your sins" (Psalm 103:12; Isaiah 43:25). Our sins are never brought up again or repeated to anybody else.

Like Joseph, I did not want anybody else witnessing or knowing what I was doing when I forgave the one who had offended me. It was all done in private. It was just us and God. That's all that needed to be there.

2. Do not make your offender afraid of you or intimidated by you. Joseph did not want his brothers to be afraid of retribution. He revealed who he was with tears streaming down his face. He wept so loudly that the Egyptians heard him from another room (Genesis 45:2). If we have not truly forgiven, we will get pleasure in seeing our offender quaking in his boots when he sees us coming. We might say to ourselves, "Good! He should be afraid!" We feel his fear is part of the punishment he deserves. But forgiveness extends a hand and says, "Come close to me; do not be afraid."

> There is no fear in love; but perfect love casts out fear, because fear involves torment. But he who fears has not been made perfect in love.(I John 4:18)

As I was talking with my offender, I assured him he needn't say anything. I didn't want him to be apprehensive or groping for words to say. I stood close with compassion and gentleness.

3. Do try to get them to forgive themselves and not feel guilty. We are tempted to go into great detail so they will remember every action and emotion. We have a big problem if we want to send people on a guilt trip. Do you know people like this? When they walk away, it's like they dumped a bucket of ice water on you. It feels terrible! But Joseph even went so far as to say, "It was God who sent me here, not you." (See Genesis 45:5.)

When we refuse to lower the boom on someone, it makes it so much easier for them to see what they have done and paves the way for them to deal with it. This makes it easier for them to offer you an apology, repent, and give their sin to God. It helps them to walk forward, leave everything behind, and build on their future with confidence and security.

4. Do allow them to save face. Allowing our offender to save face is carrying the principle of true forgiveness a step further. Saving face means salvaging one's dignity and self-esteem. It is the refusal to make the other person feel guilty. It is hiding a person's error so they won't be embarrassed in front of others. You will make a friend for life by letting them save face.

This is exactly what God does for us. He lets us save face by causing our past, no matter how bad, to work out for our good. When we can put ourselves in the offender's place, it's easy to let them save face. If we were in their shoes, we too would want to save face. When we see ourselves as we really are, we will have to admit that we are just as capable of committing the same sin as anyone else.

That day I truly wanted to allow my offender to save face. It was quite an embarrassing sin for him after all. We both knew what had occurred. It wasn't about getting every detail right and naming

115

everything for what it was. This saved him much embarrassment, emotion, guilt, and shame. When you allow your offender to save face, all parties can walk away contented, at peace, and able to move on.

5. Do protect your offender from his greatest fear. Can you imagine how Joseph's brothers felt after the truth had been revealed? The account in Genesis 42 tells us they had become agitated and apprehensive when Joseph had earlier accused them of being spies. They spoke among themselves, unaware that Joseph could understand what they said: "We are truly guilty concerning our brother, for we saw the anguish of his soul when he pleaded with us, and we would not hear; therefore this distress has come upon us" (v. 21). So when Joseph finally revealed his true identity, his brothers' fears probably increased exponentially. They feared the worst. What kind of trouble would their offense bring down upon their heads in this strange land? Beyond that, would Joseph make them go back home and tell their aging father the sins they had committed?

But sin that is under the blood doesn't need to be told to anybody except God. Joseph did not order his brothers to return home and admit their sin to Jacob. Instead, he told them to tell their father he was alive and wanted to take care of his family during the rest of the famine.

> Haste ye, and go up to my father, and say unto him, Thus saith thy son Joseph, God hath made me lord of all Egypt: come down unto me, tarry not: and thou shalt dwell in the land of Goshen, and thou shalt be near unto me, thou, and thy children, and thy children's children, and thy flocks, and thy herds, and all that thou hast: and there will I nourish thee; for yet there are five years of famine; lest thou, and thy household, and all that thou hast, come to poverty. And, behold, your eyes see, and the eyes of my brother Benjamin, that it is my mouth that speaketh unto you. And ye shall tell my father of all my glory in Egypt, and of all that ye have seen; and ye shall haste and bring down my father hither. (Genesis 45:9–13, KJV)

Some may think the brothers should have been forced to confess their sins to Jacob. But this information would have burdened their father with an impossible load of bitterness against his other sons. This would have been detrimental to the mind and health of a man of his advanced years. Joseph was very wise and fair with his decision.

We must protect our offender by letting it be known only to the people who must know, such as our counselor or accountability partner. The only exception to this is a case that involves criminal action.

6. Do treat forgiveness as a lifelong commitment. We don't forgive one day, then return to pick up the offense the next day. After their father had passed away, Joseph's brothers were once again afraid of Joseph. They were afraid the brother whom they had victimized had been biding his time until after their father's death to wreak vengeance on them for their sin.

> When Joseph's brethren saw that their father was dead, they said, "Perhaps Joseph will hate us, and may actually repay us for all the evil which we did to him. (Genesis 50:15).

Joseph wept when he saw that his brothers doubted him.

> Joseph said unto them, "Do not be afraid, for am I in the place of God? But as for you, you meant evil against me; but God meant it for good, in order to bring it about as it is this day, to save many people alive. Now therefore, do not be afraid; I will provide for you and your little ones." And he comforted them and spoke kindly to them. (Genesis 50:19–21)

The secret of his brothers' betrayal that Joseph had kept for more than seventeen years still held good. He continued to keep that secret until his dying day.

> True forgiveness is a lifelong commitment. We don't forgive one day, then return to pick up the offense the next day.

We must never reveal an abuse so that our offender can live free from fear. True forgiveness is a lifelong commitment. I told my offender the wrongdoing was under the blood. The offense was gone, washed away like water under the bridge. God's blood had covered it all and so must I.

God never brings our sins back to haunt us. Satan may try to bring them back; we may try to bring them back; but God will not. There is never any doubt or fear after God has forgiven us.

7. *Do pray for your offender to be blessed.* True forgiveness includes a final step: you must pray for your offender to be blessed. Think about the magnitude of this. You are praying, "God bless my offender. Show him or her mercy and grace. I give them to You, God!" When you pray for your offender this way, it's hard to get upset with them. It's difficult to feel ill will toward them. And it's a lot harder to think about what they did to you; instead, you will be thinking about how God will bless them.

The benefits of true forgiveness are mind boggling. But you can accomplish this only through prayer and the power of God. You are Christlike and under His covering and protection when you follow these principles. True forgiveness will change your life!

Let me encourage you today. *Forgive*! It will set you free!

Chapter 15

Restitution

Journal: *It will take time to right all of my wrongs . . . I know it won't happen overnight.*

> Then it shall be, because he hath sinned, and is guilty, that he shall restore that which he took violently away, or the thing which he hath deceitfully gotten, or that which was delivered him to keep, or the lost thing which he found. (Leviticus 6:4 KJV)

Restitution is a biblical principle, and, sadly, it is one that is not often followed. For example, many untrue and destructive "facts" are revealed in the midst of gossip. Gossip has the power to destroy people, institutions, and organizations. People have been hurt to the very core. Yet how often have you seen an offender go back to the people and places where they scattered the slander and make right what they said wrong?

Has someone ever said anything false about you? Maybe the last person they told said none of it was true, but instead of coming to you and making restitution for spreading false information, the gossiper just let it drop, as if hoping it would disappear into thin air.

The saying "right is might" is true. Truth always seems to find its way out in the open, but it takes time. And it never seems to happen according to our timing. Some people have waited years for truth to come out.

Have you ever noticed that lies about people travel much faster than the truth? One phone call about a sinful act someone committed, and within the hour it has spread all over the world! News of miracles doesn't even travel that fast. This shouldn't be.

In the New Testament, we have the wonderful example of Zacchaeus. Jesus visited in this tax collector's home and ate dinner with him. This riled many people, and they began to murmur against Jesus for hobnobbing with sinners.

All of a sudden, "Zacchaeus stood, and said unto the Lord; Behold, Lord, the half of my goods I give to the poor; and if I have taken anything from any man by false accusation, I restore him fourfold. And Jesus said unto him, This day is salvation come to this house, forsomuch as he also is a son of Abraham. For the Son of Man is come to seek and to save that which was lost" (Luke 19:8–10, KJV).

From Zacchaeus's confession, we understand that
- he had been guilty of defrauding people,
- he was remorseful over his past actions, and
- he was committed to making restitution.

Zacchaeus saw his need for God that day and repented. Beyond making a public confession of his wrongdoing, he also pledged to make restitution for those wrongs.

Genuine repentance leads to a desire to make wrongs right. I must caution you, though, that the idea of "whenever possible" is crucially important to remember. There are some crimes and sins for which there is no adequate restitution. Having said this, there should be some form of restitution made that demonstrates repentance.

God takes restitution so seriously that in Exodus 22:1–14, He commanded a person who could not accomplish restitution to sell himself into slavery.

> If a man shall steal an ox, or a sheep, and kill it, or sell it; he shall restore five oxen for an ox, and four sheep for a sheep.
>
> If a thief be found breaking up, and be smitten that he die, there shall no blood be shed for him. If the sun be risen upon him, there shall be blood shed for him; for he should make full restitution; *if he have nothing, then he shall be sold for his theft.* If the theft be certainly found in his hand alive, whether it be ox, or ass, or sheep; he shall restore double.
>
> If a man shall cause a field or vineyard to be eaten, and shall put in his beast, and shall feed in another man's field; of the best of his own field, and of the best of his own vineyard, shall he make restitution.

If fire break out, and catch in thorns, so that the stacks of corn, or the standing corn, or the field, be consumed therewith; he that kindled the fire shall surely make restitution.

If a man shall deliver unto his neighbour money or stuff to keep, and it be stolen out of the man's house; if the thief be found, let him pay double. If the thief be not found, then the master of the house shall be brought unto the judges, to see whether he have put his hand unto his neighbour's goods. For all manner of trespass, whether it be for ox, for ass, for sheep, for raiment, or for any manner of lost thing, which another challengeth to be his, the cause of both parties shall come before the judges; and whom the judges shall condemn, he shall pay double unto his neighbour. If a man deliver unto his neighbour an ass, or an ox, or a sheep, or any beast, to keep; and it die, or be hurt, or driven away, no man seeing it: then shall an oath of the LORD be between them both, that he hath not put his hand unto his neighbour's goods; and the owner of it shall accept thereof, and he shall not make it good. And if it be stolen from him, he shall make restitution unto the owner thereof. If it be torn in pieces, then let him bring it for witness, and he shall not make good that which was torn.

And if a man borrow ought of his neighbour, and it be hurt, or die, the owner thereof being not with it, he shall surely make it good. (Exodus 22:1–14, KJV, emphasis added)

God was not advocating slavery when he said, "If he have nothing, then he shall be sold for his theft." However, those words lend insight into the way God views restitution: restitution is more important to our spiritual wholeness than our civil freedom.

Here is a New Testament example of restitution:

If you bring your gift to the altar, and there remember that your brother has something against you, leave your

gift there before the altar, and go your way. First be
reconciled to your brother, and then come and offer your
gift [of worship to the Lord]. (Matthew 5:23–24)

This passage contains the serious implication that God will not
accept our worship if we have any unreconciled relationships, or for
which we have not made our best effort to reconcile. This means if
we aren't willing to make it right and haven't put our best effort into
making it right, we have no business worshiping the Lord.

I wonder how much unity among God's people there would be if
these verses alone were carried out. I can't remember a time at
church when someone came to me and made something right.
Wouldn't it be wonderful if when we walked in the church door and
saw people with whom we had issues, if either we or they would
make it right before church even started?

Consider mine affliction, and deliver me: for I do not
forget thy law. Plead my cause, and deliver me: quicken
me according to thy word. Salvation is far from the
wicked: for they seek not thy statutes. Great are thy
tender mercies, O LORD: quicken me according to thy
judgments. Many are my persecutors and mine enemies;
yet do I not decline from thy testimonies. I beheld the
transgressors, and was grieved; because they kept not thy
word. Consider how I love thy precepts: quicken me, O
LORD, according to thy lovingkindness. Thy word is true
from the beginning: and every one of thy righteous
judgments endureth for ever. (Psalm 119:153–160, KJV)

Like the fruit of the Spirit, restitution is never a requirement to
gain salvation; it is a result of our salvation. "Fools mock at making
amends for sin, but good will is found among the upright" (Proverbs
14:9, NIV). Restitution should set us apart from the world and those
who are not Christlike.

During our recent evangelistic travels, a pastor's wife shared with me a great story on restitution. Her husband had been into the drug scene in his younger years before coming to know the Lord. They married later and were called to pastor in the town where he had been involved with drugs. While in this lifestyle he had borrowed money from several different people and never paid it back. He said he couldn't pastor in a town where he owed past debts to the people he might someday be pastoring. The debt was still owed, and it would be remembered by these individuals. So he and his wife worked hard and scrimped and saved the money he owed. It wasn't easy, but they eventually paid it all back.

> If we have done wrong to anyone, we should never ask God to forgive us until we are willing to make restitution. – Dwight L. Moody

The bottom line is restitution. When you truly repent, you must bring restitution to every wrong you possibly can. For me restitution was a process—a long process. It was very painful and involved lots of people, friends, family, a church, and an organization. I had done things and said thing I would never be able to take back.

There were many agonizing days of trying to remember everything I did and said in order to make all false things true. As I came to this point in the process I was so broken and dead to my flesh that when my eyes were opened to how much damage and carnage I had created, I was grief stricken, lethargic, and numb. To be honest, if I had had a gun, I would have used it on myself and been gone for good. I really thought what I had done was so horrible that I would never get over it. I didn't want to have to face anybody; I didn't think I had the courage.

You see, I walked out of the house that cold day in February 2014 believing all the wrong things. In a few short days, our home was gone, the church my beloved husband pastored was gone, our income was gone, and my husband was no longer leading the men's ministry. In a matter of a few days, the actions and statements I had committed and said caused my soulmate to lose everything. So you understand the reason I say that some things cannot be restored. I was devastated to think I had done this much damage and would never be able to fix some of it. All I could do was start working on the things I *could* fix. I had to somehow make some sense of what had happened and allow God to strengthen and heal me.

As mentioned in previous chapters, people with BPD have thoughts and feelings that seem to be so real that no one can convince them otherwise. That's one reason why BPD is almost impossible to overcome. I had let anger and false assumptions build until they exploded all over the place. My thought processes and reasoning had gone haywire.

> I struggled with the fact that my search for restitution would reveal my BPD for all the world to see. I was embarrassed to the very core. I cringed at how people would label me. I didn't want everyone to see my hurt, pain, anger, selfishness, and all the other flaws.

I struggled with the fact that my search for restitution would reveal my BPD for all the world to see. I was embarrassed to the very core. I cringed at how people would label me. I felt like I was being exposed. I felt like my thoughts were written on a chalkboard so everyone could read them. I didn't want everyone to see my hurt, pain, anger, selfishness, and all the other flaws.

People with depression are labeled, even though there are many interpretations of "depression." Yes, since that awful time God has healed me, but back then I was still working through the process of forgiveness, restitution, and healing. I had to be very careful how I went about restitution in order not to set my healing back or trigger something in my emotions that I wouldn't be able to handle.

I started restitution a little bit at a time with some family and close friends, letting them know the truth about the situation, taking the blame off of them, and making restitution. That was really hard. The first time I let it be known what had really happened, I was an emotional wreck the next day, wondering if this person would look at me in an unfavorable light. Would they still love me? But I knew that even though the bad things I had done were tied to an emotional disorder, I knew I had to make things right. I had truly repented and was determined to cover and reach everyone to whom I had said anything untoward. I wanted everyone to know the truth.

Stan Gleason, my pastor, helped me tremendously. I am using his name because I want to give honor where honor is due. I sent a letter to the district board and to every church member where we had formally pastored. Pastor Gleason and Vani Marshall helped me in this effort, making sure everything was appropriately said and done. To them I am grateful.

I know I don't have to tell you the extent to which I went to make things right, but I'm doing it to let you how strongly I believe in restitution. If we are truly sorry and have repented, it must show, and people must see we are sincerely sorry and taking action to right the wrongs.

It grieves me that some, after being told the truth, would rather believe a lie. I can never go back and change something like that. It further grieves me that I can never make full restitution to my beloved husband. It grieves me that the tainting of my character may never be restored in the minds of some. I cannot fix the looks and the stares; I cannot fix the thoughts people still have even though the thoughts are untruthful. All I can do now is step into the future. God has kept me and restored me with great healing. It is my consolation to know that before God I am forgiven, restored, and blameless. My pastor, Stan Gleason, said, "It's one of the greatest miracles I've ever seen in the full restoration of a couple's marriage and ministry."

To be blameless means there are no grounds—or basis, or reason—for accusation because you have made every effort to correct or to reconcile in truth. In this sense a blameless person is irreproachable. He takes the initiative to be transparent with everyone. He can be held up to the light of truth and found to be completely clear because he has confessed it all. Just because he is blameless does not mean he has never made a mistake; but as far as he is able, physically, materially, and spiritually, he has done everything within his power to acknowledge where he was wrong, to correct it where possible, and to make any appropriate restitution to restore fellowship.

After you have done all you can do in your circle of responsibility, the only thing left is to stand still and leave the results of your efforts with God.

Chapter 16

The Healed Me: I'm Walking in the Light

Heal me, O LORD, and I shall be healed; save me, and I shall be saved: for thou art my praise. (Jeremiah 17:14, KJV)

Journal:
April 22, 2015

Hello Vani,

You asked me to read Psalm 91 and God would do something wonderful in my heart. Today I was listening to Lee Stoneking as he addressed a meeting at the United Nations. All of a sudden I felt God speak to me that He was going to deliver me from BPD and that I was going to write a book about my journey to complete healing. I have felt this for several years, and now and then people would tell me I was going to write a book, but it never occurred to me what it would be about.

I also feel that you, as my counselor and friend, will have a big part in this book. You have studied BPD for several years and are quite knowledgeable about it. I'm not sure how it will all come together, but I will just keep walking and let it unfold.

I wanted to share this with you because you said God would do something for me, and He did.

Love you, Jodie

I remember this very moment. I was in the laundry room standing in front of the dryer taking out the clothes when God spoke to me. From that day until today, January 17, 2018, it has been a faith-filled, healing journey. I am excited and thrilled to think about how great my God is and what He has done for me!

As I reflect on the past four years, I see many days of excitement, healing, and victory. But there also were days when I had to force myself to put one foot in front of the other, believing God was doing a work of healing in my life. I had to press on toward the day of complete healing.

In September 2012, Tony and Karen Bailey had come to our church. Brother Bailey had told me, "You will be writing a book, and it will be real soon." He added, "You are going to have great faith!" These two things simmered in the back of my mind for years.

Both Vani Marshall and Stan Gleason encouraged me to write this book as well. To me it was affirmation of what Tony Bailey had said. I know this is the book God wanted me to write, but at the time I had no clue it would be a book of a miraculous healing God did in my life.

And the "great faith" Tony Bailey mentioned? I learned that to acquire great faith you have to go through hard times. How could you get faith any other way than seeing God do the miraculous in your life and experiencing all the changes that made a believer out of you?

The saying goes, "No pain, no gain." BPD was the most painful chapter in my entire life. But I am excited about the healed me, the person God created me to be! God miraculously renewed my mind and healed my heart.

> You know if course, where this other world lies hidden.
> It is the world of your own soul that you seek. Only
> Within yourself exists that other reality for which you
> Long. I can give you nothing that has not already its
> Being within yourself . . . all I can give you is the
> Opportunity, the impulse, the key. I can help you to
> Make your own world visible. That is all. –Herman
> Hesse in *Steppenwolf*

> "Choose your actions, or your actions will choose you."
> –Anonymous

My healing was not instantaneous; it came about little by little, one layer at a time. It was a long, arduous, painful journey, but I wouldn't have had it any other way. Underneath each layer, there was new insight, new vision, new goals, and new perspective, until I saw the new me.

I think God heals in this manner for two reasons: (1) We can experience each layer and the effort it takes to work through our healing. It's more like traveling by car instead of supersonic transport. It gives us a chance to adjust, realign, learn, and grow. (2) If healing of this magnitude came all at once, it would be hard to handle. I don't think I could have; I would have been in total shock.

My healing occurred over a three-year period, and, truthfully, God is still continuing to heal me. Your healing will be different because everyone is unique. Everyone has their own story to tell. But I say, "You can do it!" Weeping only lasts for the night but, joy comes in the morning!

For me, it was a fight for survival. With tears streaming down my face I would beg, "God, help me to understand what truth is, and please place a hedge of protection around my mind. I plead Your blood over my mind." Sometimes it was hand-to-hand combat with the enemy; other times it was a retreat for a much-needed rest to give my wounds time to heal. This was always a good time to reflect on what I had learned. I found out that the heat of battle is a refining process. Every time you emerge, more gold is shining through. But I had to look for it. I had to stay focused on getting well and thinking positively.

The battle is not for the undecided or unsure. You have to be determined you are going to win. You must tell yourself you are going to win, even when you don't feel it and it looks impossible. With God, all things are possible!

Yes, I can say God healed me from BPD, but it took effort on my part. He expected me to learn what I could do to help myself. That's why I say it is so important to seek the guidance of a professional apostolic counselor as well as an accountability partner.

As I walked into complete healing, all aspects of my life changed drastically. I feel like a totally different and free person. I'm amazed at my new attitudes and Christlike responses. I sometimes will stop after an incident and marvel, "Wow! That was an easy, pleasant response!"

When we are healed, we don't have to wrestle with our feelings and thoughts before they come out of our mouth. They will come out healed, Christlike, gentle, and true. The ugly filter of abuse, rejection, and abandonment is gone. In its place is a clean, clear, and Christlike filter. Praise God!

We are not responsible for how we came to be or how we grew up. But as adults we are responsible for the person we have become and for everything we do and say. It is much easier to hold others responsible for our behavior. But if we continue to do so, we are merely puppets dangling on the strings, manipulated by our abusers. Who wants to live like that?

Imagine you're standing before the King of kings on Judgment Day.

He asks, "What was the reason for this or that behavior of yours, this or that reaction of yours?"

You answer, "It wasn't my fault! *They* made me do it" or "It's because of what they did to me!"

> I'm healed! All things have become new. I know who I am in Christ. The miracle was wrought by the mighty hand of God, my Deliverer.

Blaming someone else means you have given up your rights and choices as an adult. That may have been your habit, but believe me, you do not want to be that person. Healing will free you to make your own choices, godly choices.

I'm healed! All things have become new. I know who I am in Christ. The miracle was wrought by the mighty hand of God, my Deliverer. You, your spouse, your family member, or your friend can be healed as well. I have faith in God and in you. You can be whole again! When you come to the realization that with God anything is possible, and you believe it with your whole heart, you are on the road to complete healing.

I knew I had to change in order to survive. But I didn't have to do it all alone. God was with me every step of the way.

Relationships

My number-one relationship is with my heavenly Father. I say "Father" because that is what He is to me. I can trust Him. He has brought me through many ferocious storms. But I have learned it doesn't matter how strong the gale is, it's a breeze for my God.

My prayer life has gone from a morning ritual to thinking, *I can't wait to say hi to Him as soon as I open my eyes.* And I learned He waits eagerly for each morning so He can commune with me. I am His child. He cares about my day, how I feel, and all my thoughts and concerns.

Now my unhealthy fears have been transformed to a healthy reverence for God. I know God is not standing over me with a club, ready to strike me as I stumble and sin, but with the gentle hand of a shepherd He gently steadies me as I waver. He pulls me to His side and tucks me under His wing.

> Keep me as the apple of Your eye; hide me under the
> shadow of Your wings. (Psalm 17:8)

God has become my first responder, because when in distress, He is the first One I call. I know He will answer and meet my need. His answer may not be what I would prefer, but I know it will be the perfect plan for my life.

The rats' nest of worry I once was has turned into a haven of calm, complete trust. I am learning to let it go and give it to God. I say "learning" because we are always a work in progress.

> Trust in the LORD with all your heart, and lean not on
> your own understanding; in all your ways acknowledge
> Him, and He shall direct your paths. (Proverbs 3:5–6)

I have learned that we cannot live one moment without God. He loves to come to our rescue. That does not mean we are weak; it means that in our weakness He is made strong. The weaker we are, the more assured we can be that it was God who stepped into the situation. Knowing our identity in Christ enables us to freely say, "I can do all things through Christ who strengthens me" (Philippians 4:13). We can win the victory with God's help and strength.

Family and Friends

I have gone from unhealthy relationships without boundaries to fulfilling relationships with boundaries of love, trust, and acceptance. During the healing process, it was essential for me to connect with healthy people who did not have major issues of their own. I was striving to be healthy, so I had to surround myself with people who were healthy.

That's why I say you have to walk away from some relationships. It is a hard thing to do, but you must do it in order to heal. If you have an addiction or are around a friend or a spouse of someone who does, it is vitally important to walk away from those relationships. Maybe these were the friends you drank with or took drugs with. The bottom line is you have to sever ties from all unhealthy people. They are viewing the world through clouded lenses. They will say and do things that will distract you, and will push you off course. If you stay connected to them, you'll tend to run to them for advice rather than your counselor, pastor, spouse, or a healthy friend or support group. Walking away is a very hard thing to do, but it must be done. Your healing has got to be the most important focus in your life, not pleasing people. Your healing is all about your relationship with God, your Healer and Deliverer.

Being around people who told me the things I needed to do to heal was a vital aspect of my healing process. Healthy people are the only ones who can truly help you in the way you need. I had a close connection with Vani Marshall, Pastor Gleason, and my 24/7 supporter, my husband, Scott. The truth of the matter is you are not always able to get ahold of your counselor or pastor, so your spouse or family member that you live with is the one who can make you or break you. My husband truly helped me in my deepest, darkest hours when no one else was there. He has truly been the one person who sustained me through the entire process of healing.

Now I no longer expect my spouse or friends to bring me happiness. The joy of the Lord is my strength! I have learned to trust people, but at the same time allow them to be human. Humans are imperfect beings. We sometimes let each other down. But God is a friend that sticketh closer than a brother. He never lets us down.

There used to be no way I could truly love anyone else as long as I hated myself. In other words, I was viewing them through the same clouded lens through which I viewed myself. Thank God, loving myself has become the norm. Loving myself (i.e., looking at myself as God sees me) has enabled me to see others as God sees them. I'm looking through a clear lens now. It is wonderful being able to give people the love they deserve, and allow people to love me. There is no greater feeling. No greater way to live.

When I didn't love myself there was no room for real intimacy and honesty. There was a wall between me and them, and I couldn't communicate. Now I can talk with my love and soulmate about anything and everything. I can look at myself honestly and openly. When I look inward, I'm no longer afraid of what I see or what I might see. If something needs to change, I no longer view it as a failure; it's just something I need to work on. Freedom comes with being able to discuss with others my shortcomings and even laugh about them. I no longer hide my faults and things I don't like about myself. Whether good or bad, I will always have things I need to work on, so why not accept myself as I am? God does! God is pleased with His creation, so I might as well be too.

I trust myself. God has given me a sound mind that enables me to make good decisions, have valid opinions, and think organized, disciplined thoughts. I'm so thankful I no longer have to flip from one world to another, changing my thoughts and opinions for each world, and then try to guess which one is right. Racing thoughts was probably one of the hardest symptoms of BPD to deal with. Thoughts, opinions, and decisions barreled through my mind at high speed, making it impossible to make a good decision. I couldn't relax and trust God; I worried all the time. If only there had been an off button to give me a few moments of peace.

If I could keep myself from thinking! I try, and succeed:
My head seems to fill with smoke . . . and then it starts
again: Smoke . . . not to think . . . don't want to think . . .
I think I don't want to think. I mustn't think that I don't
want to think. Because that's still a thought. Will there
never be an end to it?" –Jean-Paul Sartre in *Nausea*

This used to be me. Thank God there are no more smokescreens. My mind is free since I learned to take every thought captive. These days, I am in control of my thoughts, feelings, and decisions. I can distinguish between truth and falsehood. My thoughts no longer scatter like buckshot; they are orderly and lucid. I no longer feel as if I am two people tossed back and forth between two decisions or answers, wondering which one is true or right. God has truly healed my mind.

The dysfunction and sexual abuse of my childhood stole away the freedom to choose my own destiny. But now, through God's help, I have taken it back. I am going to succeed and be what God intended for me to be and go where He wants me to go. I'm so excited about what God has in store!

Stress

Any kind of stress used to send me into a tailspin. The harder I tried to cope, the faster I spun. All I could do was wait for the crash. Now I've learned to be strong and depend upon God. He walks right beside me through tough times. I can handle a higher stress level without breaking. I am anxiety free. I can stay levelheaded and do what needs to be done. I trust myself because I trust God.

Perspective and the Mind of Christ

My perspective about life has entered a new dimension. I know I'm going to make it. With a renewed mind I can see something good in everything and everybody without even trying. My natural response is to look at things from a positive perspective. "Weeping may endure for a night, but I'm glad I still have my joy!"

Having a positive and uplifting perspective is having the mind of Christ. Striving to have the mind of Christ every day is a win-win endeavor. Our first thought as we wake up in the morning should be, "I'm going to make the best of this day. I'm going to have a great day in You, God! Thank You for this day and everything You have done for me!"

Having a healed and free mind brings so much peace to you. People enjoy being around your quick smile and beautiful, positive, healed heart. The glory of God shines through your countenance.

No More Dissociation

Dissociation used to be my constant companion. I learned at a very young age to dissociate from sexual abuse and other disturbing situations. It was my coping mechanism of choice. I could block out pain, trauma, or abuse by going to a make-believe world surrounded by a high wall. I totally checked out. I was at home, but the lights weren't on. Once dissociation has been learned, it is almost impossible to turn around.

I remember when I was a pastor's wife in a conversation with a saint, and they would say, "Sister Smith?" I would retreat into a trance while I was standing there saying, "Yes . . . yes . . ." My head and mind were in a fog. I couldn't think or articulate my thoughts. This also caused a lot of stress and frustration between my beloved husband and me. Many times there would be a trigger and other times it seemed to happen out of nowhere.

Praise God, it does not happen anymore. The "new me" can contribute to a conversation anytime and anywhere. I feel liberated—the lid is off the box; the jail cell is open; my chains are gone. I have told my husband, "I wish I had the words to explain how it feels to be free in my mind. It is truly like I am a totally different person. I thank my God for freeing my mind." This is truly a miracle from God!

Self-Awareness

Being aware and acknowledging what was going on was a huge step toward my healing. If you are unaware that your thinking process is not right, you don't know it needs to be fixed. As I sat in Vani's office and explained to her the two sides of my thinking process and being unable to tell which was wrong and which was right, she said, "People with BPD can't see what you're seeing! They can't acknowledge the discrepancy because it's impossible for them to see it. Jodie, this is a miracle!" As time passed, God helped me to continue not only to acknowledge my faulty way of processing thoughts and to become more knowledgeable about the process, but He also enabled me to conquer it in the name of Jesus.

I thank God every day for the miracle He has done in my life. If you were to ask Vani Marshall to sum me up in one word, she would say, "Miracle."

Chapter 17

The Borderline and Their Caregivers
By Vani Marshall

Certainly, one cannot diagnose someone without evaluating them, but many times the descriptions people give me of their significant other, parent, child, or friend leads me to wonder if the advice seeker is dealing with a Borderline. Below is the description of the nine criteria of Borderline Personality Disorder (BPD) according to the fourth edition of the *Diagnostic and Statistical Manual of Mental Disorders*:

1. Frantic efforts to avoid real or imagined abandonment (not including suicidal or self-mutilating behavior covered in criterion 5). The fear of abandonment is the Borderline's personal "nightmare."
2. A pattern of unstable and intense interpersonal relationships characterized by alternating between extremes of idealization and devaluation.
3. Identity disturbance: markedly and persistently unstable self-image or sense of self.
4. Impulsivity in at least two areas that are potentially self-damaging (e.g., spending, sex, substance abuse, reckless driving, binge eating [not including suicidal or self-mutilating behavior covered in criterion 5]).
5. Recurrent suicidal behavior, gestures, or threats, or self-mutilating behavior.
6. Affective instability due to a marked reactivity of mood (e.g., intense episodic dysphoria, irritability, or anxiety usually lasting a few hours and only rarely more than a few days).
7. Chronic feelings of emptiness.
8. Inappropriate, intense anger or difficulty controlling anger (e.g., frequent displays of temper, constant anger, recurrent physical fights).
9. Transient, stress-related paranoid ideation or severe dissociative symptoms.

Many people who have BPD also have other concerns, such as depression, eating disorders, substance abuse—even multiple personality disorder or attention deficit disorder. It can be difficult to isolate what is BPD and what might be something else. Again, you need to talk to a qualified professional.

DSM-IV Definition of BPD
BPD is marked by a pervasive pattern of instability of interpersonal relationships, self-image, affects, and marked impulsivity beginning by early adulthood and present in a variety of contexts, as indicated by five (or more) of the following:

(1) Frantic efforts to avoid real or imagined abandonment. Note: Do not include suicidal or self-mutilating behavior covered in criterion 5.

(2) A pattern of unstable and intense interpersonal relationships characterized by alternating between extremes of idealization and devaluation. This is called "splitting." Following is a definition of splitting from page 10 of the book *I Hate You—Don't Leave Me* by Jerry Kreisman, MD:

> The world of a BP, like that of a child, is split into heroes and villains. A child emotionally, the BP cannot tolerate human inconsistencies and ambiguities; he cannot reconcile good and bad qualities into a constant coherent understanding of another person. At any particular moment, one is either Good or EVIL. There is no in-between; no gray area....People are idolized one day; totally devalued and dismissed the next.
>
> Normal people are ambivalent and can experience two contradictory states at one time; BPs shift back and forth, entirely unaware of one feeling state while in the other. When the idealized person finally disappoints (as we all do, sooner or later) the Borderline must drastically restructure his one-dimensional conceptualization. Either the idol is banished to the dungeon, or the Borderline banishes himself in order to preserve the all-good image of the other person.

Splitting is intended to shield the BP from a barrage of contradictory feelings and images and from the anxiety of trying to reconcile those images. But splitting often achieves the opposite effect. The frays in the BP's personality become rips, and the sense of his own identity and the identity of others shifts even more dramatically and frequently.

(3) Identity disturbance: markedly and persistently unstable self-image or sense of self.

(4) Impulsivity in at least two areas that are potentially self-damaging (e.g., spending, sex, substance abuse, reckless driving, binge eating). Note: Do not include suicidal or self-mutilating behavior, already covered.

(5) Recurrent suicidal behavior, gestures, or threats, or self-mutilating behavior.

Affective instability due to a marked reactivity of mood (e.g., intense episodic dysphoria, irritability, or anxiety usually lasting a few hours and only rarely more than a few days).

(6) Chronic feelings of emptiness.

(7) Inappropriate, intense anger or difficulty controlling anger (e.g., frequent displays of temper, constant anger, recurrent physical fights).

(8) Transient, stress-related paranoid ideation or severe dissociative symptoms.

Dissociation is the state in which, on some level or another, one becomes somewhat removed from "reality," whether this be daydreaming, performing actions without being fully connected to their performance ("running on automatic"), or other more disconnected actions. It is the opposite of "association" and involves the lack of association, usually of one's identity with the rest of the world.

There is no "pure" BPD; it coexists with other emotional illnesses, the most common of which are mentioned in the following list:

1. Post traumatic stress disorder
2. Mood disorders

3. Panic/anxiety disorders
4. Substance abuse (54% of BPs also have a problem with substance abuse)
5. Gender identity disorder
6. Attention deficit disorder
7. Eating disorders
8. Multiple personality disorder
9. Obsessive-compulsive disorder

Statistics about BPD/ BPs comprise
- 2% of the general population,
- 10% of all mental health outpatients,
- 20% of psychiatric inpatients,
- 75% of those diagnosed are women, and
- 75% have been physically or sexually abused.

Borderline Personality Disorder is characterized by a recurring, long-standing pattern of having unstable relationships with others— whether they be romantic relationships, friendships, or relationships with family members. The condition is marked by an effort to avoid abandonment (regardless of whether it's real), and impulsivity in decision-making. People with BPD often swing from one emotion to another easily and quickly, and their self-image changes just as often.

If there's an overarching defining characteristic of someone who suffers from BPD, it is that they often seem like they are ping-ponging back and forth between everything in their life. Relationships, emotions, and self-image change as often as the weather in reaction to something happening around them, such as stress, bad news, or a perceived slight. They rarely feel satisfaction or happiness in life, are often bored, and filled with feelings of emptiness.

The term "borderline" means in-between one thing and another. Originally, this term was used when the clinician was unsure of the correct diagnosis because the client manifested a mixture of neurotic and psychotic symptoms. Many clinicians thought of these clients as being on the border between neurotic and psychotic, and thus the term "borderline" came into use.

Advice to Caregivers

How should I structure the home environment? People with BPD benefit from a home environment that is calm and relaxed. All involved family members (including a boyfriend or girlfriend) should know not to discuss important issues when the individual is in crisis mode. Stop to take a breath yourself when they do become emotionally reactive. It's also important not to center all discussions on the disorder and setbacks. Conversely, it's important not to place too much emphasis or praise on progress, or an individual may begin to self-sabotage. People with BPD should have opportunities to talk about their interests and thoughts about the news, family events, and other leisure activities. Take the time to laugh at a funny joke or eat dinner together several times a week. The less an individual feels like his or her mental illness is under the spotlight, the more opportunity they have to explore other aspects of themselves.

How can I communicate effectively during a crisis? When a loved one becomes reactive, they may begin to insult you or make unfair accusations. The natural response is to become defensive and to match the level of reactivity. You have to remind yourself that individuals with BPD struggles to place themselves in a different person's perspective. They struggle to gauge what is a minor issue and what is a full-blown catastrophe. They interpret your defensiveness as not being valued.

Instead, when they become reactive, take the time to listen without pointing out the flaws in their argument. Try not to take it personally. If the person does point out something you could improve or have done wrong, acknowledge their point, apologize, and suggest a way you can improve on the matter in the future. If the individual feels like they're being heard, the crisis is less likely to escalate. However, if the conflict rises to the level where an individual is throwing a full-on tantrum or threatening you, it's best to walk away and resume the conversation when they are calmer.

What if they threaten to hurt themselves? A crisis is escalating if a person with BPD begins to threaten to harm themselves. Sometimes self-harm signs may be less overt, such as scratching the skin, eating less, coloring or shaving off hair, or isolating from others. These actions represent the person's inability to express their emotions verbally. Recognizing early signs can help prevent an emotional crisis from becoming more serious or requiring medical or psychiatric attention.

Be aware that you don't put the idea into someone's head by asking about self-harm or suicide. Instead, invite the individual to talk about their emotions and allow yourself to gauge whether professional assistance is necessary. All threats of suicide should be taken seriously. Even if the behavior is attention-seeking, it can result in serious harm or even death. However, that doesn't mean you have to call 911 every time an individual speaks about hurting themselves. This sends the message that they have an enormous amount of power over all arguments. Instead, ask your family member what they would feel most comfortable doing when they threaten injury. They might want to speak with their therapist, call a hotline, or walk with you into an emergency room. Allowing them some amount of agency in deescalating a crisis can help calm out-of-control emotions.

What other strategies can reduce conflict? Listening and reflecting can be the most effective strategy in communicating with someone with BPD. Though you might disagree with every word that is spoken, listening is not the same as agreeing. It is simply acknowledging a person's emotions and perspective. Ask open-ended questions that encourage them to share, such as "What happened today that caused you to feel this way?" or "Tell me about how your week is going."

Statements of reflection and summarization can also help an individual feel heard. For example, if your son shares that he thinks you value his sister more than you value him, you can say, "You feel that we don't love you as much as your sister." The temptation to argue and point out their bias will be present, but just remind yourself that reflecting is not agreeing. This type of communication is not about winning an argument or being right. It's about helping your family member feel heard and deescalating conflict.

What can I do when I feel overwhelmed? Because a family member with BPD may not be able to provide the empathy and self-awareness necessary for a relationship, it's vital to have other supports in your life. Carve out time to spend with friends and engage in leisure activities. If you need to talk about the experience of living with someone with a mental illness, excellent resources can be found in support groups, mental health professionals, religious leaders, and your doctor. You also should consider how to involve other family members in the care and support of someone with BPD. No single person should be responsible for communicating calmly and responding to crisis situations. The more people who know effective strategies for responding to the individual, the less often crises will erupt.

Will they ever completely recover? Unlike with physical illness, recovery has a different meaning when it comes to mental health. Recovery does not imply the total elimination of symptoms, the lack of need for medication or therapy, and functioning comparable to persons without the disorder. Recovery from BPD looks like fewer threats of self-harm, reduction of frequency of emotional outbursts, and a decrease in the intensity of reactivity. Relapse may occur, but crises will resolve quickly and you will feel more prepared to handle the situation. In turn, your loved one will feel encouraged to take small but steady steps toward a fuller and healthier life.

To help both the Borderline and particularly the caregiver, spouse, child, or parent of a loved one with BPD, I recommend the book *Stop Walking on Eggshells: Taking Your Life Back When Someone You Care about Has Borderline Personality Disorder* by Paul T. Mason and Randi Kreger. Here are some tips from the book with some of my own advice thrown in:

(1) Stop "sponging" and start "mirroring"; that is, some of those involved with Borderlines tend to soak up the Borderline's pain and rage and think this is helpful, but in reality it is like filling up a black hole of emptiness and nothing is good enough. You can try to placate the Borderline and work hard to give them love and care, but it is never enough. Instead, reflect the painful feelings of the Borderline back where they belong—with the Borderline.

(2) Stay focused and observe your limits. Show by your actions that you have the bottom line. Communicate the limits clearly and act on them consistently. Protect yourself and your children by removing them and yourself from the situation. For example, if a Borderline flies into a rage and starts accusing you of things you did

not do, tell him or her that you will be taking the kids out until they calm down and you can talk later.

(3) Ask the Borderline for change. Figure out your personal limits (get help from a therapist if needed) and communicate these to the Borderline in a clear manner. However, ask for changes in behavior, not necessarily for changes in feelings; that is, you can ask them to change the behavior of yelling at you, but don't tell them not to be angry.

That, I think, sums it up, but the damage I have seen on victims of those who have BPD is not something to be taken lightly. People say that those with BPD can change, but oftentimes they wreak havoc on their spouses, children, and/or parents, and the abuse lasts a lifetime. Children of those with BPD have trouble in future relationships by seeking out the love of the Borderline that they could never get or by avoiding people in the future for fear of more emotional blackmail. Spouses of the Borderline seem devastated and often end up with lives of quiet desperation or in the throes of accusations in court. Parents end up believing that they are inadequate and incompetent. None of it sounds promising.

Acknowledgements

I can still hear her words as her sweet little face with eyes of kindness looked into mine:"Jodie, write a book about your healing. There are no other books out there of someone being healed of BPD. Do it. Don't wait."

Vani Marshall is one of the strongest ladies I know. She is anointed and powerful. She believed in me and encouraged me throughout my healing journey. She counseled me like no other. We had many God moments as I lay on the floor in her office sobbing, crying out to God. If it weren't for her godly and professional counseling, this book would not be. I am truly humbled that she agreed to write a clinical chapter in this book for me. Vani Marshall, I cannot thank you enough for your work, prayer, encouragement, and energy.

My dear, sweet husband and soulmate, Scott, has been my constant companion. He has seen me at my worst and still loved and believed in me. From the beginning of this project, he helped me to see I was capable of writing a good book. He sacrificed many hours taking up the slack so I could write. He helped me with research, offered ideas, and recommended sources. My husband is my number-one fan. He is the wind beneath my wings. Baby, I love you deeply, and I just don't have the words to thank you enough. My love to you!

My pastor, Stan Gleason, has been a great support from the very start. My husband and I met with Brother Gleason for lunch one day to get his blessing and okay to write this book. He has helped to guide me with suggestions and concerns along the way. He is more than a pastor; he is a true friend. Brother Gleason, thank you for trusting and believing in me. I am honored you agreed to write the foreword of my book. Blessings to you!

My longtime friend, Tony Bailey, is one of the kindest men I know. Just a few short years ago, he sat on the front pew at our church, looked me in the eye, and said, "You're going to be writing a book. It's gonna be real soon." Tony, your prophecy has come true, even though I didn't dream it would turn out to be this kind of book. Thank you for all your prayers and the friendship you have shown to me.

Thank you to my prayer team that covered me in prayer for many months: Susie Adams, my sister who applauded, encouraged, and believed in me; Sandy Axton, a dear friend with whom I could laugh for hours and who always had a listening ear and a kind spirit; Linda Wyatt, a sweet and steady friend who loved me no matter what; Donnietta Kuebler, a caring friend who was always sensitive to how I was doing and felt honored to help pray for this endeavor; and Kay Maxwell, a friend who could out-work anybody but still took the time to pray for me as I wrote this book. Thank you, ladies, for your many hours of prayer. Without prayer this project couldn't have been written. I needed the strength of your prayers as I walked through my past once more, and I needed God to anoint me and give me the words to say.

Thank you, Pat Bollmann, for all your hours of editing this book. I still remember the first conversation we had. I read a few short paragraphs to you over the phone, and you said, "You have the potential to be a good writer." I was so excited and blown away. That was my first encouragement on some actual material. I knew at that point that I could do this. Pat, you helped me tremendously with this project. Thank you for making me feel like I really had what it took to write and publish a book.

Kaitlin promised to be my promoter and seller of this book. She can sell anything. She has charisma and enthusiasm and a colorful personality. She even suggested she might wear a T-shirt with graphics on the front saying, "Buy my mom's book!" Thank you for your excitement and eagerness to help me, Kaitlin. I love you, my sweet and only daughter.

To Austin, my youngest and fun-loving son, thank you for the occasional, "I'm happy for you, Mom," and thanks for all the "I love you's." Your optimistic, gentle spirit always fills the room. You have the ability to connect and relate with anyone. Love you, Austin.

I still remember the night my sweet friend, Susan Holman, took the time to sit with me in her living room and listen to me pour my heart out about this book. She gave me the encouragement I needed for that time and place. She gave me ideas, as she herself is also a writer. Susan, thank you for pouring into me. I used some of your ideas in this book.

Suggested Reading

The Angry Heart: Overcoming Borderline and Addictive Disorders
By Joseph Santoro, PhD

The Wounded Heart
By Dr. Dan B. Allender

I Hate You—Don't Leave Me: *Understanding the Borderline Personality*
By Jerold J. Kreisman, MD, and Hal Straus

Total Forgiveness
By R. T. Kendall

Stop Walking on Eggshells: Taking your life back when someone you care about has Borderline Personality Disorder by Paul T. Mason, MS, and Randi Kreger

Made in the USA
Monee, IL
23 June 2023

36602968R00085